COLLECTION OF SHORT STORIES AND NEWSPAPER & MAGAZINE ARTICLES

by

Ruth Welburn

Published by Ruth Welburn

Welburn, Ruth (Nellie Ruth), 1941-

Collection of Short Stories
And
Newspaper & Magazine Articles

ISBN 978-0-9865322-3-8

Author Ruth Welburn

Ruth Welburn
185 — 911 Yates Street
Victoria, British Columbia
V8V 4Y9

Cover Design and Book Layout by Iryna Spica of
SpicaBookDesign

To Marie Wilcox
Your generous spirit and kindness will always be
remembered.

Table of Contents

NEWSPAPER & MAGAZINE PUBLICATIONS

Fever—
An Ancient and Beneficial Response to Infection

For years healthcare professionals considered fever to be undesirable and diligently sought to reduce it. This led to the ubiquitous and indiscriminate use of fever reducing drugs in hospitals and in homes. But is fever a bad thing? Could nature have been right after all? Is there a benefit to be gained from the very symptoms we so diligently seek to annihilate?

Fever earned its bad reputation partly because it is symptomatic of an infectious disease and partly because it causes discomfort to the patient. Reducing the fever was thought to be synonymous to treating the infection. It is now thought that quite the opposite is true.

Indeed, fever may be beneficial to our immune system. In a 2003 Bulletin issued by the World Health Organization, Heinz F. Eichenwald points out that "fever represents a universal, ancient and beneficial response to infection." The fact that fever, despite its enormous energy requirement, is found as part of the immune response in all mammals strongly suggests that fever has critical evolutionary value. Eichenwald concludes that suppression of fever "under most circumstances has few if any beneficial effects. While on the other hand some harmful effects have been shown to occur as a result of suppressing fever." He unequivocally discourages the widespread use of fever reducing medications.

In a 2007 issue of Microbiologist, Green and Hoption-Cann explain that fever is more than just an increase in temperature; it is a very complex, natural immunological response to infection and triggers the production of white blood cells and molecules that fight the infection. Fever increases the metabolic rate by 30 to 50 percent. In addition, the accompanying chills double or triple the metabolic rate. This higher metabolic rate supplies the substantial energy needed to mount an immune response without compromising the energy supply for normal cellular activity. Fever also causes blood to circulate faster which allows white cells to reach the site of infection quicker, and it speeds up the elimination of toxins from our system. Increased body temperature can also hinder the growth of viruses and bacteria and interferes with their ability to produce toxins.

One notable benefit of febrile infections is that they possess some hidden mechanism within the body's immune system that can regress or cure tumors. Since the middle of the 20th century, there has been a surge in cancer in the developed world. Before the elimination of many severe febrile diseases, fever was Nature's defense against cancer. In the late 19th century, a surgeon by the name of Dr. William Coley discovered this fact when he realized that some inoperable tumors spontaneously regressed following acute infections such as scarlet fever, rheumatic fever, diphtheria, typhoid, influenza, amoebic dysentery, smallpox and erysipelas. If the fever was high enough and of long enough duration, patients could sometimes live out their lives cancer free.

Today some types of cancer are treated by stimulating the patient's natural immune system to mount an attack on the tumour. One example of this treatment, known as "immuno-therapy," is the use of a weakened form of tuberculosis called BCG to treat superficial bladder cancer. BCG has become increasingly regarded as the most effective treatment for the removal of residual tumours following surgery. The bacterial suspension is administered directly into the bladder cavity via a catheter. It is not thought to have any anti-tumour effect, but it induces an inflammatory reaction that triggers a response by the immune system that indirectly affects tumours by attracting white blood cells and cytokines to the area. The cytokines change the environment in the bladder causing it to inhibit further tumour growth. In some cases, BCG induces flu like symptoms with fever and chills that enhance the anti-tumour action. This treatment has resulted in complete tumour regression.

A recent report at a 2010 ASCO (American Society of Clinical Oncology) suggest that fever has a beneficial side effect to immunotherapy. Researchers from Aarhus, Den-mark suspended the routine use of fever reducing drugs in patients receiving immunotherapy to treat metastatic mela-noma. They found the therapy was more effective when the patients were allowed temperature up to 41° C (105.8° F).

There is a mounting body of evidence that indicates it is folly to interfere with the intricately designed mechanism of fever. Maybe we should think twice before taking fever reducing medication and just allow fever to run its course.

❖

Published in Common Ground Magazine
Nov 5, 2010

The Virtues of Infectious Disease

As a microbiologist with a master of science degree and 30 years of experience in university research labs in the fields of microbiology, virology and infectious disease, the harsh press given to bacteria and viruses really bugs me. With last year's hype over H1N1, the hysteria around these most ancient of all life forms on Earth rose to new levels.

There is folly in the mindset of regarding all disease causing bacteria and viruses to be all bad. In some cases they can provide enormous benefit to our immune system, a view that is rapidly gaining favor among health care professionals.

In our quest to eradicate disease altogether, we seem to have lost sight of the fact that we are part of the interconnected web of life and that our immune system has evolved in that intricate context. What is the price of this?

Some diseases cause a febrile reaction, commonly called "fever". Fever has earned a bad rap of its own. However, a 2003 *Bulletin of the World Health Organization* asserts that fever represents an universal and ancient response to infection. The article points out that fever, despite its enormous energy requirement, is found to be part of the immune response in all mammals.This strongly suggests that fever has some essential evolutionary value.

Fever is more than just an increase in temperature; it is a very complex natural immunological reaction to infection and triggers a chain reaction in our bodies. Barascos et. al. reported in a 1987 issue of the *Canadian Journal of Physiology and Pharmacology* that fever, along with accompanying chills, doubles or triples the bodies metabolic rate. That supplies the substantial energy required to mount an immune response without compromising the energy the rest of the body needs. Secondly, fever stimulates the body to produce a whole raft of components needed to fight the disease. Furthermore, fever causes our blood to circulate faster, thus increasing the rate at which disease fighting components of our immune system reach the site of infection.

One noteworthy benefit of acute febrile infections is that they have been found to shrink or cure tumors by triggering a hidden mechanism within the body's immune system. Since the middle of the 20th century, there has been a surge in cancer in the developed world. Before the advent of antibiotics, modern hygiene practices and elimination of severe childhood diseases, severe febrile infections were nature's defense against cancer.

In the late 19th century, a surgeon, Dr. William Coley, discovered that some inoperable tumors spontaneously regressed following acute infections such as scarlet fever, rheumatic fever, diphtheria, typhoid, influenza, amoebic dysentery and small pox — most of which we now inoculate babies against. Nature is always in a fine balance. If that balance is altered by such conventional methods as immunization, antibiotics, fever-reducing medication or stringent aseptic practices the immediate benefit gained will eventually be offset by nature. There will be payback time.

No one would argue of course that we bring back the plague, polio, smallpox or cholera, but are we too quick to take anti-viral medications or fever-reducing drugs for non-life-threatening infections?

Even mild febrile reactions have a beneficiary role to play as is demonstrated in the case of polio. Before the 1890's, non-paralytic polio was endemic among infants, but the disease was mild. For thousands of years, because of poor sanitary conditions, most infants were infected with the poliovirus in the first six months of life. Infants receive passive immunity from their mothers while in the womb, and this protection lasts until the baby is about six months old. Because of this passive protection, the babies that were infected with the poliovirus suffered only mild fever, while at the same time, this infection provided the individual with a lifetime immunity to polio.

By 1900, the poor were infected at an early age, but the clean, middle class was susceptible to the more dangerous paralytic polio. Paradoxically, advances in hygiene and sanitation defeated nature's way of immunizing mankind against polio.

Progress in the fight against infectious disease has come a long way in the last 200 years, but have we gone too far in seeking to eradicate any infectious disease that causes any discomfort? Is it necessary to vaccinate all healthy people against influenza?

Many health care professionals are asking is there a benefit to be gained from the very diseases and symptoms that we so diligently seek to annihilate.

We need to take a closer look at ways to work with nature and not against it.

◆◇

Printed in the *Winnipeg Free Press*,
December 10, 2010

Coley's Toxins

The Hidden Cancer Treatment from the Past

High mortality rates from cancer remain today even after fifty years of research with modern treatments. This has sparked a renewed interest in a treatment from the past that has proven highly successful against advanced cancer.

In 1891 Dr. William Coley developed one of the most effective anticancer treatments in medical history, yet it is not widely known or used today. Coley's Toxins was the main cancer therapy for 70 years. Remarkably, it had a success rate of 67% or greater for all patients with advanced, inoperable cancers of the breast, ovary, cervix, and uterus, as well as with bone sarcoma, Hodgkin's lymphoma and leukemia. More than 100 scientific papers describe case histories of these successes.

The therapy uses killed bacterial preparations to induce a high fever in patients with malignant tumors. Such preparations can cause complete regression of both extensive non-invasive and invasive cancers. Many standardized cancer treatments not only fail to produce lasting cures but also interfere with spontaneous natural regressions. For example, radiation and chemotherapy cause permanent damage to the immune system and impair natural protection against cancer. Coley's vaccine, on the other hand, works with Nature enhancing the immune system; it has a higher success rate of eradicating cancer and does not cause permanent damage to the immune system.

Coley's treatment program is patterned after natural body defense mechanisms. Dr. William Coley stumbled onto one of the most important discoveries ever made in cancer research. Frustrated by the loss of a patient to bone cancer, he methodically searched the records of patients with cancer or leukemia. To his surprise he observed that inoperable tumors spontaneously regressed following acute febrile infections such as scarlet fever, rheumatic fever, diphtheria, typhoid, paratyphoid, gonorrhea, syphilis, influenza, smallpox, yellow fever, leprosy, amebic dysentery, tuberculosis and erysipelas. If the infection was severe enough and of long enough duration patients went on to live out their life cancer free. If the cancer was in the late stages and the patients suffered only a mild infection the tumors regressed only partially.

There has been a surge in the incidence of cancer in the developed world since the middle of the twentieth century. Before the advent of antibiotics, modern hygiene practices and the elimination of severe childhood diseases, severe febrile infections were Nature's defense against cancer. Healthy people carry hundreds of microscopic pockets of cancer throughout their body. Each of these cancer pockets damages the surrounding tissues producing miniature "wounds". Macrophages, the large white blood cells of the immune system, are given the task of identifying foreign cells that cause infections. They are the intelligence agents for the immune army. Once the army is informed that the body is under attack it will mount a full scale offensive, kill and remove the invaders. But the immune system also plays the role of disaster relief at home. If intelligence signals that it has identified wound tissue the army goes into repair and heal mode producing rapid growth factors that promote healing. The macrophages must distinguish between an invading foreign interloper and a distressed fellow countryman. Normally they would recognize tumor cells as foreign but they are fooled into seeing them as "wound" because of the damaged tissue that surrounds them. The immune system now actually promotes the growth of the tumor. However if the cancer patient contracts an acute febrile infection the immune system's priority is to mount a full scale offensive against the invading bacteria and in the process it removes the tumor cells.

Acute febrile infections are Nature's way of protecting against cancer. Nature is always in a fine balance. If that balance is altered by such conventional methods as the use of antibiotics, fever reducing medicine or stringent aseptic practices the immediate benefit gained will eventually be offset by Nature. There will be payback time. We should work with nature not against it and not lose sight of the fact that mankind is part of the interconnected web of life.

Coley's Toxins is not approved for use in Canada. In 1963 Health Canada set new stringent rules for approving drugs. The medical-industrial-regulatory-complex of the time did not recognize the extensive data on Coley's Toxins. Health Canada "grandfathered" only those drugs being produced by a drug company at the time. Coley's is a natural bacterial product and cannot be patented therefore was not being manufactured. The 70 years of extensive data showing Coley's to be a safe and effective treatment were not recognized.

At present, Coley's is available in clinics in the United Kingdom, Germany, the Bahamas, South Africa and Mexico. With renewed interest and clinical trials set to begin in Canada, Coley's and related immune therapies may well be the preferred cancer treatment of the future.

A Pilgrim's Quest

A few years ago, a cryptic feeling flitted across my mind. I had a sense of something ancient and unknown within me. I wondered what it was exactly and wanted to make contact with it and explore it, but I didn't know how. The thought was as elusive as the butterflies that flit in and out of view all along the Camino.

Some time later, I learned that my son's mother and father-in-law had walked a pilgrimage in Spain. This was the first time I had ever heard of the Camino, and I knew instantly that if I were ever to understand this ancient part of me, it would be on this pilgrimage.

On my seventieth birthday, my son gave me a round trip ticket to Europe, and I was off on my quest to connect with what I eventually came to recognize as my unconscious mind.

To prepare myself for the inner journey, I read Carl Jung's autobiography—*Memories, Dreams and Reflections*—and I discovered that Carl Jung, himself, had gone on much the same search that I was on.

For a couple of weeks before my trip, I house sat for a friend on Thetis Island. I spent the time alone reading my book and walking. I slept well, and I began to dream. In one dream, I had a vivid image of a distinctive cross. The cross had three fleurs-de-lis and was mounted on a sword. I felt that if I saw this cross somewhere along the way, the place might have some significant meaning, and I watched for it on churches all along the Camino.

In late August, I flew into Paris, and after spending a few days at the Lascaux Caves, travelled to Bayonne where I caught the train to Saint Jean Pied-de-Porte in southwestern France. This train was packed with pilgrims—all headed for the Camino. I felt an immediate common bond, and I knew that even though I travelled solo, I was not alone. We were a community of souls bonded together in common purpose and on an inner journey—a group of seekers, all starting at the same place and walking in the same direction—all forsaking our controlled, busy, anxious lives, all with eyes and minds wide open—inquisitive—open to what we might discover along the way.

We were all aware of the challenging outer journey that was an integral part of our path. The physical journey would be arduous, but it was a necessary part of our quest. It would serve to keep us grounded. The sages of old must have understood that the physical and spiritual aspects of man are intricately interconnected. The very act of walking on the natural contours of earth somehow anchors us in reality—the term "grounded" took on a new meaning. This grounding frees our mind to delve into the wellspring of the unconscious within. It gives us space for reflection.

Carrying all my possessions on my back provided a sense of complete self-reliance and cut the tethers that bound me to the consumer driven society from which I came. I was free to walk. Perhaps because I was in a strange land or because of my sense of adventure, I found myself living in the now. I was keenly aware of my surroundings. My senses had opened like a flower at the peak of season. I was aware of the smells and the majestic views; I could feel and taste the air around me; I felt the heat from the sun; I stopped to watch the buzzards soaring high in the sky, the butterflies as they darted in and out of view, the expansive fields of sunflowers and always the silhouette of fellow pilgrims up ahead; I listened to the rhythmic beat of my footsteps and the poles against the earth; I felt the weight of my backpack, and I was aware of my breathing as it kept pace with my feet.

I walked alone, yet I was not alone, I was part of all my surroundings—in fact the word "alone" lost all meaning. I was certainly a part of the stream of pilgrims—all in motion, all moving westward toward the Holy City. The thought of turning back was unthinkable. There was a strong force drawing us ever forward toward Santiago. Once, I got off on an alternative route and missed the town I had planned to stop at and replenish my water supply. I didn't have enough water to take me the long distance to the closest town ahead (I think about 10 kilometers), and I was sitting on a rock contemplating the unwelcome thought of walking back four kilometers and the consequences that would have, when a young women wearing a long skirt, sandals and bandana stopped and asked me if I was all right and did I have enough water. She filled my water bottle and then was off like she had done nothing important. That act of kindness did more than provide the essential water I needed for survival; it made me feel the need to give something back to someone else along the way. And as I once heard someone put it so fittingly—the positivity spirals upward along the way.

The mechanical act of walking leads the mind through the outer layer of conscious thought and into the wellspring of the unconscious below. You can't hurry, you have the weight of the backpack, there is an incredible distance to travel, and you want to stop along the wayside and observe. The concept of time falls away and gives space for reflection. I long wondered why we dream, but I think now that dreams are the only contact we have with our unconscious, and I think that this contact might be as vital to humans as food and water.

Days of uninterrupted being in the now, in awareness, with our senses, allows our inner wisdom to direct us and guide us on a path that would lead to a more fulfilled life—on a path of enquiry and of self-exploration, and as in our outward journey, it enhances our senses so that we can see things with clarity. It even allows us to see thing with senses we did not know we had. One very magical and wonderful evening in the cobblestone square of the Cathedral, under a clear starry night complete with full moon and street quartet playing Russian renaissance music, I saw the scene as an artist might. Everything seemed surreal. I felt that I was seeing my surroundings in much the same way that Van Gogh must have seen the sky the night that he painted *Starry Night*. He could never have conveyed what he saw with words.

The last leg of the Camino wends its way through the mist-shrouded valleys of Galicia, the Celtic region of north-western Spain. Here, I felt a strong sense of connection to my Irish roots. There were many pilgrims from Ireland on this section, and as I looked into their faces and talked with them, I felt I belonged. I learned to love and accept my red hair and freckles, my Irish countenance, my size and personality. I learned to accept myself for who I was and love myself.

Reaching Santiago was bitter sweet. I slowed down the last two days, just to prolong the experience, and I walked with four women that I had met along the way. It was a different experience from walking solo. The time for reflection was gone, but we partied and exchanged stories and really enjoyed ourselves. We walked into Santiago together and made it in time for the noon mass at the cathedral. But somehow I wasn't ready to end my pilgrimage, and after a few days' rest, I went on to Muxia and Finistere. But that felt like an anticlimax. I had always prided myself on "taking the road less travelled by," but what came to mind was—perhaps there is a reason why it is less travelled.

However, the destinations of Muxia and Finistere were wonderful, and it was at a Priscillian church in Muxia that I first saw the cross that I had seen in my dream. I was thunderstruck that I had actually found it—but why in Muxia? I asked a fellow pilgrim about the cross and she said matter-of-factly, "Oh, that's the Cruz de Santiago. You must have seen it on the cathedral in Santiago." But it had been pouring rain when we walked into Santiago, and I wasn't looking at anything outside. I just dashed from one cover to another and ran up the steps of the cathedral into the church. I was not to see that cross until later on my return to Santiago on that magical night under the stars on the cobblestone street in Cathedral Square. I was dancing in the moonlight with a very special man who I met on my last night in Santiago when I looked up at the majestic cathedral and saw the Cruz de Santiago silhouetted against the night sky.

I told my fellow pilgrim about my dream, and she told me that Carl Jung says that dreams go forward and backward, and that, in my dream, I was remembering something I had not seen yet. I'm still pondering those concepts.

Returning home, I realized that—as with the outer journey—with the inner journey, there is a strong resistance to going back. I've heard it said that the Camino has no end. Once we dive into the mysteries of our unconscious and experience the soul awakenings, there is a strong desire to be in motion, to move ahead towards a more fulfilling life. This inner journey cannot be directed by the conscious mind—the conscious mind needs to step aside and allow the unconscious to guide the way. I felt a desire to return to church—the Unitarian Universalist church here in Victoria, BC—and the message of peace and tolerance resonated with me. I heard the excellence in the music provided by our music director, choir and accompanist, and I was drawn to be part of this community. I joined the choir and, at age 70, I took my first voice lesson. The whole music experience has been better than I could ever have expected.

I'm still seeking, and I don't want to turn back to life as I knew it, before the Camino.

❖

Published in the 2013 edition of
Confraternity of Saint James Bulletin
No 124

Winter Solstice
at Newgrange Ireland
Stone Age Observatory?

walked along the path leading from the Visitor Center at Newgrange to the Passage Tomb and paused on the bridge over the River Boinne. The water babbled softly as it curled its way compliantly around the vast high mound that obstructed its journey to the Irish Sea. Fish jumped upstream, and a family of ducks glided effortlessly on the river's surface. Across the meadow, cows basked lazily in the afternoon sun. Upstream a man cast a line into the swirl. Butterflies flitted in and out of view, and I could hear but not see the birds chirping in the trees at the water's edge. The aroma of the forest completed the enchantment. I had arrived.

I had come to Europe to walk in the steps of the Stone Age people who had built megalithic monuments all over the British Isles and Brittany. I am writing a historical fiction set 5200 years ago and wanted to understand just who these enigmatic people were and how they could have achieved such incredible feats of architecture and why. Whimsically, I had dreamed of traveling back in time to observe them first hand. This was better than I could ever have hoped for. This scene I stood in had not changed since the day Newgrange was built. In my mind, I stepped into the world of my book.

As I walked along the path, the wooded area abruptly gave way to an area of bulletin boards where people waited for buses to transport them up the hill. I wished I could walk the two kilometers to Newgrange, but it is now an UNESCO heritage site and carefully controlled. I watched the country-side pass by my window — the same pastoral scene of eons ago. From time to time through the trees, I got a glimpse of the sun glinting off the white quartz exterior of the imposing structure strategically positioned at the highest elevation in the area. Covering more than an acre of land and sitting at the center of the world's largest amphitheater rose 13.5 meters high. It was just as awe-inspiring as it must have been to it's astronomer-builders.

When we reached our destination we were shepherded up to the main entrance passed massive horizontal stones that ringed the base of the structure.

An intricately engraved stone lay across the entrance which had been reconstructed to allow access to the passage chamber. We were led 19 meters through a corridor of standing stones to a cruciform inner chamber with an amazingly beautiful three meter high corbelled roof that remains water tight today. As if this was not impressive enough, we were treated to an re-enactment of what happens on Winter Solstice when the light from the rising sun enters the roof-box located above the entrance and illuminates the chamber.

I was struck by the corbelled roof, the chamber's cruci-form shape and the stone placed at the entry of the tomb. Had Neolithic architecture influenced Christianity?

After exiting the tomb, I walked around the circumference. Of the 96 kerbstones at its base, several had inscriptions carved into them that had survived over 5200 years. My heart skipped a beat. Had the ancients left messages written in stone? I was particularly drawn to the artwork on kerbstone 52. It seemed to echo the entrance stone. Both had a vertical line down the middle to the right of the famous tri-spiral. I was informed that the Solstice sun fell on the vertical line of the entrance stone at Winter Solstice and also illuminated the tri-spiral on a standing stone inside the chamber. It also aligned with the vertical line on K52 which is located on the far side of the mound. It is believed that the curbstones and the stones that line the passageway and chamber were positioned before the mound was built.

Intrigued by the artwork, I scoured the literature looking for interpretations and learned that the engravings all pertain to things astronomical—a recording of what the Stone Age people were studying at the site and their findings. The Irish archaeoastronomer, Paul Griffin, reported in the Washington Post that one of the stone carvings at Loughcrew is a drawing of the solar eclipse of November 30, 3340 BCE — the world's oldest known recording of a solar eclipse. James Swagger, in his book, The Newgrange Sirius Mystery, writes "Newgrange occurs to me and many others to be a Stone Age university of observational astronomy. The heavily featured artwork there seems to all to be a teaching platform." Swagger makes a convincing case that Newgrange was built to study earth's wobble.

On my return visit in the fall, it seemed obvious that this was indeed a place of highly advanced astronomical study. It is now recognized that Newgrange was more than a passage tomb. "Temple of the Stars," is a more fitting description as it appears to have been a place of burial, ritual, art and observational astronomy.

Ruth Welburn is the author of *The Devil's Ruse* and soon to be released historical fiction, The Land of The Watchers. She is also the mother of RASC NB member David McCashion.

❖

SRAC NB RASC Volume 19, Issue 1—page 3
www.horizon-vol_19-no_01-RASCNB
Contact: authorruthwelburn.com
Contact darren@extremeireland.ie for information on an archaeoastronomy tour of Ireland's ancient past.

A Heritage Gem:
The House that Captured the
Innkeepers

sit sipping a cup of tea on a Sunday afternoon in the large country style kitchen of the Heritage Gem B&B. Sandra, a petite genial redhead sits across the table and chats enthusiastically about the many interesting guests that have passed through the Inn and left a lasting impression on her and her husband, Larry—the innkeepers of this charming old home.

As we chat, it is clear to me that the Inn is not just a business to them—it is a part of their identity. There is a sense of fun about them as they talk about the original owner of the home, Captain Walker, and his Japanese wife, Sat Fukuyama, who died and was buried in England before Walker built the house in Victoria. Larry and Sandra have forged a bond with the Captain and his wife even though they never met. Well—not in the flesh anyway, but their ghosts reside on the second floor, dart in and out of bedrooms and hover over Sandra as she plays the piano.

Larry reflects that if he could travel back in time. The one thing he would like to do is sit on the hillside and watch the house being built. Sandra speaks tenderly about the

Japanese woman that she never knew in person, but whose ghost wishes to join her husband here in Victoria and will not rest until her remains are brought from England and laid in Royal Oak cemetery beside the Captain. From the minute Sandra greeted me at the door, I felt wrapped in the warmth and grace of the place. The spacious foyer opens into a splendid parlor to the left, while a staircase on the right leads to the second floor. The rich tones of the hardwood floors, the elegance of the décor, and the meticulous attention to detail in every room radiate a love and peace that indeed can be felt.

Larry's book is a wonderfully warm sketch of a heritage property in Victoria, but it is first and foremost a love story. You feel the love Larry and Sandra have tor their heritage home, their cats, ghosts and particularly for the world weary travelers who stop by and share their life's journey with the friendly innkeepers. Oh—and grumps are not allowed. The criticism I have of the book is that the pictures do not capture the true magnitude and ambiance of the house.

After reading the book you will want to spend a night at "The Heritage Gem."

A book review of Larry Eugene Gray's novel: *A "Heritage" Gem*
written for *Writers' Choice Reviews*

Quiet Outlet for Dark Memories

Ray W. Lane, 93, recounts ugliness of war in his book, *In Chariots of Iron*, the personal adventures of a soldier in a Canadian armored brigade

My uncle never talked about the war. To those around him, it was as though those years were a forgotten part of his memory, locked away somewhere in the hidden recesses of his brain.

The reality is that he lived those horrific experiences silently every day. The memories haunted his dreams and intruded into the very fabric of his waking life.

Eventually, he discovered that painting could provide an outlet for the dark unrelenting recollections of this period of his life.

In a series of six paintings, Ray Lane found a subtle way to express what he could not put into words. A watercolor painting he did appears on the front cover of his book, *In Chariots of Iron*.

"I had a haunting memory of this small village of Ifs with its shattered church tower that stuck with me long after the evening I passed through it," he writes.

Lane finally broke his silence 60 years after his return from the battlefield when he started writing down his memories for his book, *In Chariots of Iron*. In it, he talks about the ugliness of the war and the trauma he still suffers today. The experiences were so burned into his memory that he recounts them with such clarity and precision that they could have happened yesterday.

He begins in 1934 as he chronicles a "war in the making," as seen through his 14-year-old-eyes. From reading his book, it becomes clear that Lane does not see himself as a hero, but rather a survivor. He humbly asserts that he wears his medals "vicariously … to remember all the men who lost their lives … and never got the chance to wear (theirs) — though earn them they did indeed!"

From Britain, he relates his experiences through the bloody battlefields of Normandy and Northern Europe until VE Day. A statement on his website reads: "Indeed, Corporal Lane got an unwelcome promotion to crew commander of his Sherman tank when the former crew commander suffered a fatal head wound."

The horror of war remained a constant companion upon his return to civilian life. He describes "the smell of the tank's diesel fumes mingled with the smell of a friend's blood as it dripped on the tank's hot transmission and cooked." Lane could "smell this mixture whenever he was near a diesel-powered vehicle."

Through his writing, Lane hopes that the reader will gain a sense of what war is really like. And an understanding of the conflict that returning soldiers live with in civilian life. He writes, "Resolve never to let your guard down to bullies like Adolf Hitler. Seek peace earnestly! War is dreadful! Thank God for all who protect us."

Lane is an Alberta boy. Born in the Calgary General Hospital, he grew up in Calgary and small town southern

Alberta. After the war, he settled in Edmonton where he lives today.

Dr. Ken Welburn, clinical director of the Ottawa Anxiety and Trauma Clinic, believes that Lane's book is important because it gives voice to the experiences of the soldiers on the front lines during the Second World War.

"Many of those experiences have (remained) silent for nearly 70 years. In spite of being unspoken, the effects of those experiences have been felt by the families of vets: nightmares, irritability, withdrawal and disconnection from others are frequent results of wartime trauma."

The silence that Lane exhibited is typical, says Welburn, who is also Lane's nephew.

"In fact, 'don't talk about it' was the position of the army at the end of the war. On return from overseas, soldiers were told: 'Look, you've been through hell and yet we won— so go home, put this behind you, forget about it and get on with having families and living your life.'" Welburn concludes, "Someone is finally talking about (the trauma of war), and I believe that Canadians will want to hear."

Ruth Welburn is Ray W. Lane's niece. He was a member of the 31st Reconnaissance Regiment in Calgary. Ruth Welburn is also the author of *The Devil's Ruse*, a historical fiction that takes place on the home front during the First World War.

Written by Ruth Welburn for *The Calgary Herald*
November 6, 2011

SHORT STORIES

Murder in Tasmania

My sister, Kate, and I were intoxicated by the very fact that we were in Tasmania. After exploring Hobart, we were on our way to Port Arthur, some sixty kilometers southeast on the South Sea, to see *the* most famous penal colony in Australia. We touched down in Adelaide two days earlier following three weeks in Southeast Asia en route from Canada. Our senses laid bare to the smells, sounds, sights and vibes of our new surroundings. Everything was an adventure. Even driving on the wrong side of the road. Turning corners, especially left hand turns, was frustrating. The windshield wipers came on every time I tried to use the turn signal.

It was late day by the time we pulled into the driveway. Mid-January hung long and sultry in the southern hemisphere. We were awestruck by the scene spread out before us—the hulking remains of the old church left with no roof and the massive vestiges of crumbling prison walls scattered through eucalyptus and angel trumpet trees against a backdrop of the South Sea—all in perfect harmony. Yet I sensed an ominous undercurrent to the place.

We hurried up the steps of the hostel. A plump woman behind the desk accepted $35.00 for our one-night stay. She seemed overly nervous, and in her eagerness to tell us about the colony, she followed us to the dorm. "Even the hostel has it ghostly——," she burbled.

Kate was impatient. "Sorry," she cut in, "but we have to run,"

We slung our backpacks onto the two remaining lower bunks and headed down the road to a nearby pub for a quick supper.

The only other patrons sat at a table close by—three young people, an American woman and two Aussie men. From their conversation, we assumed that the woman had been hitchhiking and they'd picked her up. She was buying them shots of liquor. As time wore on, their language got louder and more sexually offensive—so bad that the bartender asked the men to stop. Finally he refused to serve them, and the three got up to leave. The guys exchanged a knowing glance, and the more obnoxious one uttered; "I wonder what she has in store for us tonight."

It disturbed us that the girl tolerated this behaviour. Kate grasped for some explanation. "She's self-destructing," she said. "Probably punishing herself to punish someone else—maybe her parents."

By the time we arrived back at the penal colony, tourists were assembling at the café on the lower area of the grounds by the continent's ragged edge. In the dying embers of the day, we gathered for the 'ghost walk'.

Like an apparition, a man cloaked in black appeared out of the crowd and began narrating. "After sunset, the darkened ruins of Port Arthur give up their secrets," he said. "You are about to witness the colony's hidden side."

My sister was delighted. She is a storyteller herself and formed an immediate bond with John, the narrator. She was quick to volunteer to be his lantern bearer, and they chatted theatrically as they led the tour. We followed, the lanterns we carried casting long shadows.

It was only dusk when we reached the ruins of the old church, but it was here, within its broken walls, we first witnessed the full moon. The soft glow of cosmic dust created an enchantment that served to accentuate the darkness in the alcoves.

John tossed a corner of his cape over his shoulder and began his story:

> "The keepers of the colony and their British families could occupy the seats inside the nave, but the prisoners, who were obligated to attend church, stood in chains in the vestibule on the side of the sanctuary. They were expected to repent their sins and feel remorse for their transgressions."

John's words were filled with compassion for the prisoners. I recalled reading that Australians consider it prestigious to find a convict from one of these early penal colonies in their family tree. Their crimes were of a political or petty nature; some owed a debt or stole a loaf of bread, some were just homeless.

I stepped into the area where the prisoners would stand, and when I did, I felt hatred so powerful and so foreign that it startled me.

Leaving the church, we passed the parsonage. Here John stopped briefly to address the group.

> "The parsonage is believed to be one of *the* most haunted buildings in Port Arthur. It was here that the vicar is said to have confined a boy born in the penal colony. The child served the jailor's family and

apparently often looked out the window. He died at age six. Some visitors claim they can see his face in the window of the cottage."

The image was clearly visible to me!

We crossed the moonlit grounds to the ruins of the main prison. Here, John turned to face us. The flickering lantern cast a ghastly light on his face. He peered out from the hood of his black cloak and recounted the dark history:

"The prison's eighty cells form the shape of a cross. Punishment was designed to subdue the spirit of the prisoners. It was based on silence, isolation, work and religious instruction. Convicts were required to wear a hood over their heads and reflect upon the crime that brought them to this place. Some languished for as many as twelve months in a cell devoid of light and sound. Unusually high rates of madness occurred. One inmate, William Riley, entered the prison at age fourteen because he had no parents. A few years later he murdered a fellow inmate—struck him three times on the head with a pickax while they were building the church. Riley was executed. Another man, William Carter, hanged himself in his cell. In order to escape, some convicts committed murder punishable by death. However, it is said that their souls were not able to leave. Mysterious lights have been seen where prisoners were confined, and some claim they've heard the screams of a boy awaiting execution."

Following that chilling introduction, John led us into the prison between the rows of cells. Through the barred windows, I could see the beauty that lay outside. The silver moon lit the grounds and seemed to provide a path over the South Sea to the edge of the world. I stepped into a cell—I learned later that it was where William Carter hanged himself—and tried to imagine what it would have been like to look out on the paradise beyond the dank confines of a cell. I found myself overcome. I couldn't breathe and frantically pushed people out of my way until I made it outside.

That was the first time I saw the Southern Cross. A man—who followed me to make sure I was all right—pointed it out. The Southern Cross was a big disappointment to me; it appeared small and crooked. Somehow, though, it seemed fitting that a cross looking down on this site should be so wretched.

By this time, we were near the end of the tour. I could see the café through the trees, when suddenly a gigantic cross loomed white in the moonlight. Flowers—some wilted, some fresh—lay on the newly disturbed earth on which it stood. I was so shocked that I cried out, "This is going *too* far. It looks like a *real* gravesite."

The man by my side seemed surprised that I didn't know. "It is," he said. "A few months ago a young man with a semi-automatic rifle opened fire on a group of tourists inside the café. He lived on a farm nearby and often delivered produce to the café. They say he suffered from feelings of social isolation. He murdered thirty-five people that day."

It was all too much for me. My fitful sleep that night was crowded with nightmares, and I woke several times in the night filled with fear and despair.

The next morning, we seemed to be surrounded by unpleasantness. The hostelier accused my sister of taking the cash jar from the kitchen, which upset Kate. Later, as we packed our car, the woman came running out to tell us that the jar was back in its place. "Just a friendly ghost playing a trick," she beamed with not even a hint of remorse for her false accusation.

Even in the driveway as we prepared to leave, two men argued heatedly over gas expenses. They slammed suitcases on the ground and swore loudly at each other. We tried to block out the nasty scene and drove away in wooden silence.

It wasn't until we reached the highway that we started talking again. We discussed how long it would take to reach Cole's Bay and if we should phone and let them know that we would be arriving late. We never again mentioned Port Arthur.

The Mists of TidyTown

TidyTown could be a village right out of a children's book. The vibrant colors of the tidy houses — red, blue, purple, yellow, cream, green, and varying shades of these — would promise a most pleasant bedtime story.

The town council does not tell the villagers what color to paint their houses, nor do the townspeople hold meetings to decide what coordinating colors to use or when to paint their houses. No, as I heard one TidyHome owner say as she watched her next door neighbor put a fresh coat of azure blue onto his exterior walls, "I wonder if it is time for me to paint my house and what color I should use."

TidyTown does have an official name, Eyeries. The people of the town take great pride in having been named Ireland's Tidiest town many years over.

Actually Eyeries is not a town at all. It is a village, as it is neither big enough nor of sufficient population to be called a town. I couldn't pronounce the name, so when asked where I was going, I would have to say, "to a town on the most southerly tip of the Bhéara Peninsula, southwest of Cork to a town with a name I cannot pronounce." Eventually I came to realized that Eye is pronounced "I" and ries is "Reez".

I arrived in TidyTown after dark one blustery night on the bus from Cork. Heavy fog and torrential rain obscured the countryside, so I didn't see the sign at the juncture where a road leads off in a gentle "S" down the hill before disappearing into the town. The road crosses a brook before entering the town and meanders past a bar, church, general store and rows of tidy houses arranged linearly along the village's only street, and ends at the post office. Although I could not see the road as it enters the town from the window of the B&B where I stayed, the houses figured prominently.

I was soon to learn there is much more to TidyTown than the sweeping coastal vistas and the houses. This remote Irish peninsula is steeped in history that threads its way through the twentieth century all the way back to Neolithic times. Hanging on the dining room wall of the B&B is the front page of the New York Times newspaper from May 8, 1915. The headlines read: "Lusitania sunk by submarine 11 miles off the southern coast of Ireland. Twice torpedoed by the German U-boat U-20 off County Cork and sank in 15 minutes."

I hadn't realized that the sinking of the luxury liner occurred so close to Ireland or how much the war must have personally affected the local people.

There were more surprises. Buried deep in the mists of this sleepy Irish peninsula, lay treasures carefully guarded from anyone who does not chance to visit here.

I had come to Eyeries to attend a writer's retreat and finish writing my book — a novel set 5000 years ago in Ireland. As I wandered the rugged hillside, I felt the Muses arise from the land. I heard the echos and felt the spirit of the ancients as they rose to live again. My writing journey had turned out to be better than I could ever have hoped for. I had stumbled onto a place that once gave inspiration to great Irish poets and writers. And—I could hardly contain my delight when

I discovered that this magical landscape held archeological treasures that date back to the time of my book, a history which is imbedded in the very enigmatic geologic fabric of the area. The ancients really were one with the land.

One lovely day when the rains had stopped and the sun was actually shining, I was invited to take a break from my writing and visit some of these places. Our first stop was the ruins of a seventh century Catholic Church and graveyard at nearby Kilcatherine. Complete with Celtic headstones and a holy well, the remnants of the church stand on a windswept hill overlooking the bay. In stark contrast to the breathtaking views, there was a hauntingly eery aura about the place. I sensed that the church caused the ancient spirits of the land a great deal of unrest.

A short distance up the road from the Kilcatherine ruins stands the Hag of Bhéara—that is if you are one to believe in Irish legends and mythology. I have come to do just that, so much so that I incorporated the Old Crone into my novel. She stands looking out over Coulagh Bay waiting for her fisherman husband to return from the sea.

Irish legend has it that the Devine Old Hag was born on the ancient festival of Sambains, it being a cross quarter day in the ancient calendar which corresponds to the day after our Halloween and known as All Hallows' Eve. She grows younger all winter, and by the spring feast of Bealtine she is a beautiful young woman. But through the summer months She loses her power and grows old again. Much like our shadow-seeing groundhog of modern day mythology, if the weather is poor on Imbolc, the hag is asleep and winter will soon end, but if it is a lovely sunny day she is awake and out collecting firewood to make winter last longer. For reasons associated with the clash of the Celtic religion and

Christianity, the Hag was turned into a pillar of stone. This has indeed been the fate of many legendary women over the ages. One I recall was turned to a pillar of salt.

A plaque by the stone explains that the Hag of Bhéara was the goddess of sovereignty. According to legend, she is as old as the oldest rock and embodies the spirit and strength of the land. She considered the arrival of Christianity a threat to her powers. One day after gathering seafood along the shores of Whiddy Island in Bantry Bay, the hag found the catholic priest, Saint Caitiarin, asleep on a bare hillock. She grabbed his prayer book and ran off, but the saint woke up. He caught her and turned her into a grey pillar-stone with her back to the hill and her face to the sea. There she stands, an enigmatic extrusion of metamorphic rock keeping vigil over Bantry Bay for her husband, God of the Sea.

The crowning glory of the day for me was the visit to the Ogham Stone and the geological anomaly surrounding it.

Off the windswept headland of the Bhéara peninsula, a thin pillar stone stands 5.3 meters high. It was thought to have been erected during the Bronze Age and sits on a circular tuft of land that is surrounded by naturally formed concentric circular ridges. I wondered if the stone formed a massive sundial and calendar during the Neolithic period. It casts a long shadow as the sun moves around the sky during the day which of course changes in accordance with Earth's journey around the sun.

The sun's shadow falls cross the ridges of concentric circles, but they were so overgrown with vegetation that it was not possible to tell whether there are other stones that align with the sun's shadow at specific times of the year.

Adding to the charm of the place, clumps of holly trees with their bright red berries and ivy growing on them surround the periphery of concentric circles. Holly and Ivy take me back to the days of the Druids.

The stone is on private farmland so we had to ring ahead for permission and leave two euros in a box. Along the side of the stone itself is an Ogham inscription. The stone itself was erected somewhere between 3000 BCE and 1200 BCE, but the Ogham markings were carved into it much later. Perhaps the first or second century AD.

I will return one day to hike the Bhéara Way around the peninsula—a chance to commune with the ancients again and restore my soul.

The Curious Case of the Writer's Retreat

t was a strange little house—weird even. The photos on the website were of the exterior of the house and the beautiful vistas of the surrounding landscape. Even photos of the rooms were of the view from the windows. So cleverly had the ad been crafted that I hadn't questioned a thing. I just had to travel to this quaint little place in a far off land and finish the book I was writing.

Being that the journey was exhausting, I stayed a couple of days in the port of entry before embarking on the twelve hour bus trip to the remote area where the retreat was located. Wanting to be fresh when I arrived at the retreat, I arranged accommodation in the village a few days prior, and the host of the B&B delivered me to the property.

That was the first time I began to feel that things might not be completely as I had expected. I had called ahead with the time of arrival, but was met by a sign on the front door which read "WRITING SESSION IN PROGRESS. PLEASE DO NOT DISTURB." The sign was permanently fixed to the door; it was not one that could be turned over with the other side saying "WELCOME." No, there was nothing welcoming about the sign. Quite the opposite. It sent the same unnerving message as do signs on gateposts that announce in large, bold, block letters: "BEWARE OF THE DOG."

Reluctant to ring the doorbell, I was trying to decide what to do when the front door opened, and the large formative figure of a woman filled the entrance. The proprietor must have seen me from her office window as I came up the walkway past the bird feeder on the front lawn. She did not greet me immediately, but after scrutinizing me briefly, said coolly, "Come in."

The porch was the size of a small elevator cage, one door opening to the outside of the house, and the other to the interior. I wondered at the purpose for this closet entrance, which appeared to have been not an original part of the house, noting that the proprietor's large body prevented any visitors from seeing into the house from the door, and if a person of smaller stature were standing there, the second door could block visual entry.

I was shown my tiny room with the trundle bed and the bathroom I would share with the occupant of the larger bedroom, told to read the house rules that lay on the desk in my room before I did anything else, then "feel free to explore the rest of the house." And just in case I had any doubts as to who was the alpha dog, the proprietor added, "The laundry room and the kitchen are off limits."

I left my bags in the room and, taking the file folder and my glasses, went to explore the house and find a comfortable nook to sit and read the regulations. The door to my room had no lock, and there were to be five other guests, but I found the expectation of trust and respect a welcome relief. Also, having to lock a door every time I entered or left the room would be a distraction.

The house was laid out in a manner so strange that the house itself had a creative energy to it. I marveled at how each area was so compartmentalized. When in one room, I was oblivious to the fact that there was any other part to the house. The field of vision was like that in a dream where the dreamer sees only the relevant people and surroundings—much as in the film, *The Last Wave,* which was filmed in Dreamtime. I remembered the cryptic words of the aboriginal shaman when asked what dreams are. "Dreams are a way of knowing," he said, and I wondered if being in a room in this house—so much like being in a dream—would help me to know what I wanted to create, if the house itself could show me a clearer image of the story I wanted to write.

The layout of the house was choppy. The door from my room opened into an alcove off a hallway which led to a foyer bounded on my right by a wall and on my left by the closed exit to the porch and the forbidden door to the kitchen. Around the corner from the kitchen was the dining room, and five steps emptied down from the entryway to a living room with a wood burning fireplace. Three chester-fields partitioned off a sitting area leaving an empty space along the edge of the room through which one must pass to access the steep, narrow stairwell that hugged the wall on its journey to a loft. The loft was cluttered with old books, but it was not like any room I had seen before in the homes of avid bibliophiles, nor was the collection of books ordinary. No, they looked more like the books you would find in the dusty recesses of a large annual used book sale—a place I love to browse in the hopes of finding a very old worn classic that might have a comment written on the inside cover by the owner who proudly owned it when it was new. It was as if the proprietor had gone to such a place, loaded up on all the free books and brought a truck load back to give the image that this was the home of a voracious reader of classic literature.

I retraced my steps from the front of the house past my room and between the proprietor's bedroom and her office to where the hallway spilled downwards into a single room, filled with brochures and bric-a-brac, through which one must pass to get to the other section of the house. This part of the house was bewildering, one might say like a labyrinth, but that does not entirely describe it. Up again on the main level, a foyer exited both onto the garden at the front of the house and onto the veranda at the back. I wanted to step out the back way and take a photo of the bay across the meadow, but that door was locked. From that landing, several doors led into rooms in the midst of a maze of stairwells leading up to secret rooms in the attic and down and around to a small galley kitchen for the use of the guests.

The dining room at the front of the house seemed to draw me, and I sat down at the far end of the rectangular table to read the rules. That was where I would work for the next two weeks. I don't know what the allure of that room was, it had no view of the water and looked out over an indistinguishable dark space that seemed not to exit beyond the boundary of the dinning room. I wondered why. Maybe it was because the living room was lower than the dining room and because of the intervening empty space behind the chesterfield. Perhaps the loft was obscured by its level or the back of a couch along its railing. At any rate, I worked in the solitude of the dining room for the duration of my stay.

At seven o'clock, supper was served at which time the cook set six places around the table, one for each of the five guests and one for the proprietor. That was when I became aware of two facts. The dining room was quite small for such a gathering. When the chairs were pulled out from the table to seat the guests, there was no room to get around the table. It was then also that I realized the shutters on the wall backing onto the kitchen opened in order to allow food to flow into the dining room and dirty dishes back into the kitchen. Although the kitchen was a forbidden room, this opening made it seem less clandestine.

The meals were sufficient, the food wholesome and varied, but I had looked forward to engaging conversation with other writers around the supper table. On the first night when the conversation descended into matters of defecation, I thought that perhaps things just took a wrong turn, but when the topics got worse each successive night — eating the Holy Prepuce, and other topics too indelicate to mention — I realized something was wrong. With the exception of the woman who was preparing a talk for a conference, and the artist who only stayed two days, I don't think the others belonged there at all. And the proprietor, although she did know her way around book layout software, did not seem to be the editor she claimed to be.

Even so, there was something about the retreat that was very conducive to writing. I would get up early and work at the dining room table until I heard the proprietor go into the kitchen to prepare breakfast. Then I would take my shower and dress for the day. Our beds were made in the morning, and we put our laundry in a basket outside our bedroom door once a week. Household chores had always seemed minimal to me, but I realized during my stay at the retreat just how much they had disrupted my train of thought. I reflected on how liberating it must be for a man to have a wife who takes care of all those details.

I was so immersed in my writing that I paid little attention to other things that seemed to be a bit off. One day Speech Writer and I were interrupted from our work and sent out for a walk against our protestations. The proprietor said she was going into town that day, but when I asked if I could get a lift to the bank, she suddenly decided she wasn't going to town after all. It seemed that she and her friends never left the house that afternoon. I wondered why. Did she have pest problems, and there was an exterminator coming that they didn't want us to know about?

Then there was the case of the hot tub. Before leaving Canada, I packed a bathing suit and had my legs waxed in anticipation of spending evenings relaxing in the hot tub on the outside deck while watching sunsets over the bay. The hot tub did exist. It sat on the back deck just as described on the webpage, but when I suggested we use it one evening, I was discouraged by everyone except the woman preparing the speech. She had also hoped to use the hot tub that night. We had discussed it on our way back from the walk we were forced to take when we tried to access the back deck from the yard but found the gate locked and bolted from the inside.

The house held other secrets as well — there was the curious case of the invisible dog for instance. At the end of my stay, a neighbor dropped by with her little boy to visit the owner's dog. I didn't know there had been a dog in the house. I never saw or heard one. The proprietor seemed uneasy with the revelation and studied me silently in the same way she did on other occasions when she seemed to have something to hide. Even through the hypnotic fog of my writing trance, that look spooked me.

But for all the intrigue of forbidden rooms…, locked doors and gates and other clandestine happenings, I wasn't really focused on the things that seemed amiss. The fact that everything was just a little off skew seemed only to add to the mood of the strange little house. It put me in a place that was not quite real, a place where I could retreat into my subconscious mind and write.

Pilars of Salt inspired by the Hag of Bheara On the most southern tip of Ireland's Bheara Peninsula stands the Hag of Bheara. If you believe in Irish legends and mythology, The Old Crone stands looking out over Coulagh Bay waiting for her fisherman husband to return from the sea. Irish legend has it that the Hag was born on the ancient festival of Sambains, It being a cross quarter day in the ancient calendar which corresponds to the day after Halloween. She grows younger all winter, and by the spring feast of Bealtine, she is a beautiful young woman. But through the summer months she loses her power and grows old again. If the weather is poor on feb 1, the Hag is asleep, and winter will end soon, but if it is a lovely sunny day she Is awake and out collecting firewood to make winter last longer. For some reason, She was turned into a pillar of stone, as has been the fate of many legendary women over millennia. One that I know of was turned to a Pilar of Salt.

Pillars of Salt

My name is Edith, but I was called Ado one time when my Sunday school teacher thought I was being too independent of thought because I asked why Lot's wife was turned into a pillar of salt. Ado was the supposed name of the nameless wife of Biblical Lot. The churchmarm warned me that it was a sin of pride for a woman to question God's decision, and that I should learn from Ado's fate lest similar punishment befall me.

But I never learned that lesson. Even though I was brought up in a devout Christian family, I continued to question, out loud or to myself, how any Christian could justify calling a pure, innocent, newborn child a 'bastard', or how rape, sexual assault and oppression of women could be so prevalent in the world I live in, or why the Bible was so full of misogyny.

So when I stumbled upon the existence of a sophisticated, matrifocal, peaceful, agrarian, Goddess worshiping culture that existed for thousands of years in Neolithic Europe — a discovery I made on a journey of self discovery that took me on an eight hundred kilometer pilgrimage across northern Spain, to Stonehenge, the Lascaux Caves, the alignments at Carnac, and to the museums, art galleries and cathedrals of London and Paris — I was driven to expose this newfound knowledge in the hopes the world would wake up and see the dysfunctional values of our male dominated society for what they are.

I couldn't wait to meet the ghosts of this remarkable ancient society, so I sold my house in beautiful British Columbia, and off I went on a two year expedition. I met people along the way who said it was impossible to know how Stone Age people could erect the megalithic structures found all over the British Isles or align the stones at Carnac. "No one will ever know," they said. But I knew differently. If I could uncover what goes on at the molecular level during my career in medical research, I could and would resurrect this long lost society.

By the fall of the second year, I was preparing to make my fourth three-month journey to Europe for some final research and to finish the first draft of my book. I decided to make my first stop a quaint little writing retreat set on a remote island off the coast of Ireland.

Being a single woman of a certain age, I received comments about how brave I was. I never felt unsafe in Europe, even in France where I didn't speak the language, but the comments caused a pride to swell in my breast for being able to navigate trains, buses and rapid rail systems of the cities and out of the way places I visited. Having lived a rather conventional life, I was totally unprepared for the epiphany that was about to be revealed to me.

My book being about the sensuous matrifocal society that built celestial sites all over the British Isles and Brittany, I wanted to take part in the winter solstice celebrations at Stonehenge and Newgrange that year. The retreat taking place over the first two weeks of December fit perfectly into my itinerary. So despite the protests of my children that I shouldn't spend Christmas by myself and I shouldn't be traipsing all over the world by myself at my age, I set out on the adventure.

Being that the journey from Vancouver to Ireland was exhausting, I stayed a couple of days in Dublin before embarking on the sixteen hour trip by train, bus and ferry to the remote area where the retreat was located. Wanting to be fresh when I arrived at the retreat, I arranged accommodation in the village a few days prior, and the host of the B&B delivered me to the property. That was the first time I began to feel that things might not be completely as I had expected.

The retreat was a strange little house, weird even. The photos on the website were of the exterior of the house and the beautiful vistas of the surrounding landscape. Even photos of the rooms were of the view from the windows. So cleverly had the ad been crafted that I hadn't questioned a thing.

I had called ahead with the time of arrival, but was met by a sign on the front door which read "WRITING SESSION IN PROGRESS. PLEASE DO NOT DISTURB." The sign was permanently fixed to the door; it was not one that could be turned over with the other side saying "WELCOME." No, there was nothing welcoming about the sign. Quite the opposite. It sent the same chilling message as do signs on gateposts that announce in large, bold, block letters: "BEWARE OF THE DOG."

Reluctant to ring the doorbell, I was trying to decide what to do when the front door opened, and the large formative figure of a woman filled the entrance. The proprietor must have seen me from her office window as I came up the walkway past the bird feeder on the front lawn. She did not greet me immediately, but after scrutinizing me briefly, said coolly, "Come in."

The porch was the size of a small elevator cage, one door opening to the outside of the house, and the other to the interior. I wondered at the purpose for this closet entrance, which appeared to not have been an original part of the house, noting that the proprietor's large body prevented any visitors from seeing into the house from the door, and if a person of smaller stature were standing there, the second door could block visual entry.

I was shown my tiny room with the trundle bed and the bathroom I would share with the occupant of the larger bedroom, told to read the house rules that lay on the desk in my room before I did anything else, then "feel free to explore the rest of the house." And just in case I had any doubts as to who was the alpha dog, the proprietor added in her North American accent, "The laundry room and the kitchen are off limits."

I left my bags in the room and, taking the file folder and my glasses, went to explore the house and find a comfortable nook to sit and read the regulations. The door to my room had no lock, and there were to be five other guests, but I found the expectation of trust and respect a welcome relief. Also, having to lock a door every time I entered or left the room would distract from my writing.

The house was laid out in a manner so strange that the house itself had a creative energy to it. I marveled at how each area was so compartmentalized. When in one room, I was oblivious to the fact that there was any other part to the house. The field of vision was like that in a dream where the dreamer sees only the relevant people and surroundings— much as in the film, *The Last Wave,* which was filmed in Dreamtime. I remembered the cryptic words of the aboriginal shaman when asked what dreams are. "Dreams are a way of knowing," he said, and I wondered if being in a room in this house—so much like being in a dream—would help me to know what I wanted to create, if the house itself could show me a clearer image of the story I wanted to write.

The layout of the house was choppy. The door from my room opened into an alcove off a hallway which led to a foyer bounded on my right by a wall and on my left by the closed exit to the porch and the forbidden door to the kitchen. Around the corner from the kitchen was the dining room, and five steps emptied down from the entryway to a living room with a wood burning fireplace. Three chesterfields partitioned off a sitting area leaving an empty space along the edge of the room through which one must pass to access the steep, narrow stairwell that hugged the wall on its journey to a loft. The loft was cluttered with old books, but it was not like any room I had seen before in the homes of avid bibliophiles, nor was the collection of books ordinary. No, they looked more like the books you would find in the dusty recesses of a large annual used book sale—a place I love to browse in the hopes of finding a very old worn classic that might have a comment written on the inside cover by the owner who proudly owned it when it was new. It was as if the proprietor had gone to such a place, loaded up on all the free books and brought a truck load back to give the image that this was the home of a voracious reader of classic literature.

I retraced my steps from the front of the house past my room and between the proprietor's bedroom and her office to where the hallway spilled downwards into a single room filled with brochures and bric-a-brac through which one must pass to get to the other section of the house. This part of the house was bewildering, one might say like a labyrinth, but that does not entirely describe it. Up again on the main level, a foyer exited both onto the garden at the front of the house and onto the veranda at the back. I wanted to step out the back way and take a photo of the bay across the meadow, but that door was locked. From that landing, several doors led into rooms in the midst of a maze of stairwells leading up to secret rooms in the attic and down and around to a small galley kitchen for the use of the guests.

The dining room at the front of the house seemed to draw me, and I sat down at the far end of the rectangular table to read the rules. That was where I would work for the next two weeks. I don't know what the allure of that room was, it had no view of the water and looked out over an indistinguishable dark space that seemed not to exit beyond the boundary of the dinning room. I wondered why. Maybe it was because the living room was lower than the dining room and because of the intervening empty space behind the chesterfield. Perhaps the loft was obscured by its level or the back of a couch along its railing. At any rate, I worked in the solitude of the dining room for the duration of my stay.

At seven o'clock, supper was served at which time the cook set six places around the table, one for each of the five guests and one for the proprietor. That was when I became aware of two facts. The dining room was quite small for such a gathering. When the chairs were pulled out from the table to seat the guests, there was no room to get around the table. It was then also that I realized the shutters on the wall backing onto the kitchen opened in order to allow food to flow into the dining room and dirty dishes back into the kitchen. Although the kitchen was a forbidden room, this opening made it seem less clandestine.

The meals were sufficient, the food wholesome and varied, but I had looked forward to engaging conversation with other writers around the supper table. On the first night when the conversation descended into matters of bodily functions, I thought that perhaps things just took a wrong turn, but when the topics got more bizarre each day, I realized something was wrong. With the exception of the woman who was preparing a talk for a conference, and the artist — the retreat was for artists and writers — who only stayed two days, I don't think the others belonged there at all. And the proprietor, although she did know her way around book layout software, did not seem to be the editor she claimed to be.

Even so, there was something about the retreat that was very conducive to writing. I would get up early and work at the dining room table until I heard the proprietor go into the kitchen to prepare breakfast. Then I would take my shower and dress for the day. Our beds were made in the morning, and we put our laundry in a basket outside our bedroom door once a week. Household chores had always seemed minimal to me, but I realized during my stay at the retreat just how much they had disrupted my train of thought. I reflected on how liberating it must be for a man to have a wife who takes care of all those details.

I was so immersed in my writing that I paid little attention to other things that seemed to be a bit off. One day Speech Writer and I were interrupted from our work and sent out for a walk against our protestations. The proprietor said she was going into town that day, but when I asked if I could get a lift to the bank, she suddenly decided she wasn't going to town after all. That was the third day of the retreat and the day after the artist was mysteriously dismissed.

Then there was the case of the hot tub. Before leaving Canada, I packed a bathing suit and had my legs waxed in anticipation of spending evenings relaxing in the hot tub on the outside deck while watching sunsets over the bay. The hot tub did exist. It sat on the back deck just as described on the webpage, but when I suggested we use it one evening, I was discouraged by everyone except the woman preparing the speech. She had also hoped to use the hot tub that night. We had discussed it on our way back from the walk we were forced to take when we tried to access the back deck from the yard but found the gate locked and bolted from the inside.

The house held other secrets as well — there was the 'curious case of the dog in the night,' for instance. At the end of my stay, a neighbor dropped by with her little boy to visit the owner's dog. I didn't know there had been a dog in the house. I never saw or heard one. The proprietor seemed uneasy with the revelation and studied me silently in the same way she did on other occasions when she seemed to have something to hide. Even through the hypnotic fog of my writing trance, that look spooked me. And—the neighbor and her little boy also had North American accents.

But for all the intrigue of forbidden rooms, locked doors and gates and other clandestine happenings, I wasn't really focused on the things that seemed amiss. The fact that everything was just a little skewed seemed only to add to the mood of the strange little house. It put me in a place that was not quite real, a place where I could retreat into my subconscious mind and write.

I gave little thought to the writer's retreat throughout the rest of my journey. So focused on wrapping up the final pages to my book, searching for a publisher and enjoying the winter solstice celebrations at Newgrange (sunrise) and Stonehenge (sunset), my thoughts were of the immediate adventure. It wasn't until months later, after I returned to Canada at the conclusion of my two year odyssey, that I was to think again about the mystery of the writer's retreat.

I drove to Vancouver and met my sister one day at the Waterfront. We walked through the trendy district, ate on decks overlooking the busy harbor filled with splendid sailboats and yachts and watched the seaplanes as they took off and came in for landing. It had been three years since we had been together and we were anxious to catch up on things. My sister is also a writer as well as a story teller, and her favorite authors are Irish, so she was anxious to hear of my sojourn in the country brimming with folklore, mythology and charm that she loves so much. I told her about the strange little writer's retreat and she, being the natural born inquisitive sleuth that she is, went home and researched some of the facts I had shared with her. Her email that night prompted me to take a closer look at the strange happenings at the retreat that up until then I had only seen as charming. She researched the name of the charity that the retreat was dedicated to supporting, and questioned the ultra conservative values of what she found.

"It looks like that the retreat was run by right wing fanatics who oppressed women and freedoms," she mused. "But that doesn't square with the spidey sense I got when listening to the strange happenings at the retreat. It actually reminded me of the women's underground railway of the seventies that was set up to move women fleeing abusive husbands."

"Oh my gosh," I said, and began blurting out incoherent sentences.

"It all makes senses now. The proprietor hated her Mormon ex-husband so bad her face flushed and her large body shook at mention of him. She had a startled look on her face when I announced that I knew of the obscure hamlet near Bountiful she mentioned thinking no one would ever have heard of it.

The artist was told two days into her stay that she would have to vacate her room to make space for a new arrival, but I never saw anyone in that room for the remainder of the two weeks. I had the feeling that I was an outsider and was being watched with suspicion. This was unusual. I usually connect with people. And the writer from New Zealand, the artist and I, were the only ones to have a pot of coffee provided with their breakfast or tea with other meals and, the bottle of wine I set on the table for the group was snatched up and left unopened and — and Oh my God, the baby bottle warming on the stove one day in the guest kitchen at the back of the retreat.

"Eh?" My sister crinkled her face at my excited outburst.

"They were fleeing abusive polygamous marriages, but still practiced their Mormon beliefs!"

"But I thought you said they were fleeing the Mormon religion."

"No, I said they were fleeing abusive husbands. Battered women often cling to their religion. They don't recognize it as an integral part of the abuse. My mother-in-law told me she could not have coped with the abuse she suffered at the hands of her husband if it were not for her faith. After a beating she would go into the bedroom and say the rosary."

"Maybe that's why you felt so passionate about writing your book." My sister was looking at me with new understanding and speaking calmly. "Perhaps you found religious values you could finally relate to. The ancient civilization of the pagans aligned with the values of the natural world as opposed to our society's artificial values." And of course, she had to invoke her favorite author. "Thomas Hardy felt that women are more in tune with nature than men," she said. "It's reflected in his writing."

I was filled with a sense of awakening.

Tales From a Woodpecker

Wack-a-wack-a-wack wails Hmi-hmo. High from his perch on the trunk of a trembling aspen, Pileated Woodpecker paused in his quest for bark beetles and carpenter ants and watched the people camped by the lakeside. Frost gnawed the golden boreal forest and brought an end to the warm fall interlude. This was his lake. The people had named it Hmi-hmoo (pronounced Ma-Me-O).

The Iyiniwok would soon be leaving to follow the bison south as they had done for the last ten thousand years. In the summer months, they camped by the lake.

Now that the berries and roots had been harvested and the wild game dried, they made ready for the winter migration. Tonight, men busied themselves with the horses and travois as women prepared the evening meal. A woman, carrying a papoose on her back, prepared bread from root flour. Crystal clear spring water boiled in a pot suspended in the center of the open campfire in front of her tipi. A young girl slipped away from the encampment and made her way down to the lake. On the beach, the girl unfastened her parfleche, pulled off her deerskin dress and waded out into the shallow waters. When the water reached her hips, she dove in and swam. "Awâsis!" her mother called, and the girl obediently returned to shore and joined her family around the fire. Tonight, the family would feast on white fish, bread, birch syrup and huckleberries.

As the setting sun cast its magic across the lake's surface, flocks of geese and ducks descended on the wetlands to the south of the lake. An old man, wrapped in a bison fur, left the campfire and walked out to the edge of the lake. His eyes fixed stoically on the lake, but they seemed to see more than the pristine landscape. The old man knew he would not see the lake another year; consumption had weakened him. His leather face showed signs of weariness. As he reflected on the changes he had seen in his lifetime, a feeling of foreboding came over him, and he worried for the future of his people. He had heard stories of strange migrants with strange animals, conveyances and customs. He had even witnessed them himself once at a distance.

The year was 1845, and at the time, the Iyiniwok were possibly the last prairie Indians to call this land theirs. But the old man knew their days were numbered. He felt the western migration pushing ever closer, and sensed the destruction it would bring with it.

But the Iyiniwok were not the only ones uneasy about the pending clash of cultures. The migrants had their own reservations about their distant wilderness destination. They knew the frontier was without law and order, and they perceived the Indians to be savages. In an effort to civilize the Indians, the Hudson's Bay Company and the Wesleyan Society of England sent missionaries west in advance of the settler. In 1840, they built an Agricultural Mission on the north shore of Hmi-hmoo Lake "to teach the Indians the secrets of established agriculture and convert them to Christianity." However as a local history of the district, *Freeway West*, reports, "a massacre at nearby Battle Lake wiped out the party and (the missionaries) were forced to vacate."

By 1869, the Canadian government prepared to send expeditionary forces to maintain law and order in the Canadian Northwest, and in 1870, Lieutenant William Butler was sent out in advance of the army as an intelligence officer. He was to report back on the Indians and advise on how to make the frontier a safer place for the settlers. Butler would travel 6,000 kilometers across rugged terrain, and his report would lead to the founding of the North West Mounted Police. In his book, *The Great Lone Land*, Butler gives a poignant first hand account of "these poor wild wandering sons of nature" and describes them as "the only perfect socialists…in the world." The Indian, he states, "holds all things in common with his tribe—the land, the bison and the moon."

In 1872, The Dominion Lands Act offered homesteaders160 acres of FREE LAND! And they came—from all over eastern Canada and Europe—they flooded into the district in search of the Promised Land.

Surveyors partitioned the land into neat parcels; settlers cleared their quarter sections and built houses. They put up fences, plowed up virgin soil, introduced domestic animals and planted non-indigenous vegetation—grains, vegetables and flowers. Roads crisscrossed the district, schools, health centers, missions and churches sprang up and postal service was established. Butler's prophecy was being fulfilled—the migrants that flooded into this "Great Lone Land" would convert the "wild luxuriance of … useless vegetation into all the requirements of civilized existence."

But it did not prove to be the land of milk and honey that the settlers had expected. The soil was poor, the growing season was short and subject to hailstorms, and the winters were long and cold. Farmers tried to grow wheat, but the conditions were more suited for hay and pasture. In a letter published in *Freeway West*, one disillusioned homesteader writes, "We… were sadly depressed when we saw what a poor, miserable-looking country it was. … Emigrants come by the hundreds but they go out as quickly as they come." Still many remained, some because they were too poor or too far from home to do otherwise.

By this time, the Cree had been restricted to a tract of land called Ma-Me-O reservation, and the few remaining bison confined to National parks. The name of the lake was changed to Pigeon Lake—a move that underscored the disconnect of the settlers with the natives. Would that they had been privy to the observations and insights of Butler. Of the Indian, Butler writes, "This River, this Mountain, this measureless meadow speak to him in a language of their own. Dwelling with them, he learns their varied tongues, and his speech becomes the echo of the beauty that lies spread around him. Every name for lake, or river, for mountain or meadow, has its peculiar significance, and to tell the Indian title of such things is generally to tell the nature of them also."

Less than a hundred years later, Hmi-hmoo rested his long tail against the trunk of a coniferous snag and feasted on beetle larvae. Wack-a-wack-a-wack he wails. A feeling of déjà vu came over him as he looked out over the lake. The pleasant scent of pine radiated from freshly peeled logs, and a one-armed man stood on the roof of the cabin he was building on the very site where the Cree had camped earlier. A woman sat in the shade of a willow nursing an infant, and a little girl ran towards a swing beside the lake. The little girl would spend many days looking out over the lake from that swing suspended between two of Hmi-hmoo's pines.

In addition to farming, the little girl's father harvested white fish from the lake, and delivered the mail. He writes in *Freeway West*, "I took on a mail route…from Westerose to Battle Lake and Yeoford, … to Crystal Springs and back, three days a week.… Sometimes the roads were very bad to say the least, and sometimes they were terrible. But there were always a few days every year when the roads were lovely. And those days made up for all the grief and woe."

But after a brief seven years, the man relocated his family to Edmonton. He writes, "(After) I lost my left arm…I had my right shoulder blade broken while skidding wood. … I was wearing a hook on my left arm and this hooked into the chain and I tried to back the team up while working in the bush in deep snow. The team bolted and dragged me a quarter of a mile… I was in the hospital in Edmonton for some time and unable to haul the mail again. … I must say the people on my two mail routes were very kind. They took up a collection of more than two hundred dollars, although many of them were very poor themselves. They sure were good-hearted people…"

Today, the farms have made way for one of Alberta's most beautiful recreational areas. A comfortable summer home now stands on the site of the log cabin—a sailboat is tied up at its dock. The pigeons are long gone, the water level is lower now and the lake is polluted, but Woodpecker's slow resounding hammering still echoes across the lake. His wild laugh booms through the diminishing forest, and the holes riddled in the trees mark his territory.

Wack-a-wack-a-wack wails Hmi-hmo, and he wonders what ever became of the little girl who used to swing out over his lake.

The wind whispers through the aspen, "She lives far over the Mountains of the Setting Sun, by the Shores of the Western Continent where she writes the Woodpecker's tale."

Three Country Miles

Gordon pulled up to Battle Lake Store with harness swaying to the rhythm of the horses' hooves that Friday morning late in May, 1932.

"Haw," he called and swung the team down to the water trough. He stepped down from the wagon and unhooked the horses.

A sorrel mustang stood by the trough, a heady scent of oats emanating from a leather feedbag that hung from her ears. Initials on the saddlebags read R.C.M.P.

Gordon clipped a mailbag between the tongs of the hook that was his left arm and lifted an empty six-pack of Coke from the wagon.

On the steps of the store, a Mountie pressed tobacco into a crease of paper and squinted into the sun.

"Morning," he called. He put the cigarette behind his ear and returned the Camel pouch to his inside pocket. "I'm told you deliver the mail in these parts. Have you seen this man?" He held out a photo.

"What's he done?"

"Gone missing." The Mountie pointed westward to a road that undulated like Christmas ribbon candy through the dense boreal forest of the Northern Alberta foothills. "Somewhere down that road. He left the camp Monday morning for what would be no more than an hour's walk to the store and disappeared into thin air. His wife was expecting him home that day, but he never arrived."

Gordon sprinted up the steps and examined the picture. "Can't say. I rarely see any of the itinerants at the camp. I just leave the mail with the cook." He turned to enter the store. "I need to sort the mail for today's run," he said. "You might ask the Reverend over at Battle Creek Baptist. He preaches at the camp once a month.

Inside the store, three men sat around a pot-bellied stove. The conversation stopped when Gordon entered, and he knew they were talking about him.

"Mornin' Murt, Elliot, Swede," he said as he filled an enamel cup with coffee from the stove.

"Mornin', god morgen," they mumbled.

Elliot had just opened his mouth to proffer his opinion on the news of the day when Edvard Munch returned to the room. "I put twenty sacks of oats in the back of your wagon, Elliot, and filled your can with kerosene. With the sack of potatoes you brought me, you owe three dollars and sixty cents. That's a lot of seed grain."

"Most is for Gimley's place. We're seeding his back forty tomorrow."

On Tuesday, Albert Gimley broke his shoulder blade while cranking his tractor. He managed to walk two and a half miles to the store, and Edvard took him to the hospital in Wetaskawin.

Gordon peered over the post-office wicket. "There's a postcard here for you, Ed, from Albert." He read out loud. "BE HOME ON BUS WEDNESDAY."

"Guess I'll be takin' care of 'is livestock for another few days," Elliot said.

"I can do that today," Gordon offered. "Goin' by there anyway."

Constable McLeod poured a cup of brew from the enamel percolator and leaned against the counter listening to the locals chew over the mystery of this year's missing lumberjack.

"If you ask me," Elliot said, "The bus driver is responsible for all three disappearances. Gus comes in here three times a week with the incoming mail and picks up any mail going out. What's to say he doesn't read it? He'd know who's planning on leaving the camp and when."

"Yah, Yah." Swede nodded. Issac Sventon was affectionately known to the local folk as Swede. "The poor sod vould be alone with Gus the whole trip back to Vetaskawin. Plenty remote forest to dump a body."

"This time of year cougars would make short work of the remains," Murt added and spit out a wad of tobacco.

"Could be that the men were attacked by wild animals, and there is no crime here to be investigated at all," Gordon interjected. "I saw a cougar on that road this spring, and last week I saw a grizzly sow with two cubs. That's why I always carry a rifle with me."

"'Spose that's possible," McLeod said, "But no one goes missing anywhere else in these woods. Yet each year for the last three years a logger, who just happens to be carrying his entire winter wages on him, disappears from that very same three mile stretch of road between the camp and the store. Someone must've seen something. That road can be seen all the way out to the meridian line except where it dips in the valleys, and the last half-mile stretch can be seen from the camp."

"And from Gimley's place," Murt added. "Talk to him when he gets back from the hospital. His cabin's at the juncture where the road turns down to the camp. He can see the whole three country miles from his place, and his favorite pastime is watching everything that happens on that road through the scope of his rifle. Nothing happens that Albert doesn't know about."

Ed was behind the counter now, and the Mountie showed him the picture. "Did this man come into the store Monday morning?"

"I don't recall that he did," Ed replied, adding "The only time we see the lumberjacks is when they arrive in the fall and leave in the spring. They work long hours so's they can return home before seeding time. Sometimes they stop to buy tobacco on their way through. I don't recall any itinerant comin' into the store Monday morning though."

"Most of the lumberjacks are farmers from around these parts," Murt said. "They leave the wife at home to do the chores, and go to the camps to earn enough money to pay the taxes on their farms and buy seed grain. Maybe, with a wad of cash in 'is pocket, he decided to get away from it all. A lot of them have been through the Great War and the '18 pandemic. Now with the great depression, couldn't fault anyone for wanting to escape it all. Maybe go out to Vancouver and get a taste of the good life for a while."

"Yes, that might happen, but in one case, not three.

The Mountie turned to Gordon. "His name is Lee Hilliard. Any mail for him?"

"No, I haven't seen that name, but I just bundle all the mail for the camp together."

"I'll take the mail to the camp today," the Mountie said. "I'm going there anyway."

"It is possible that the men never left the camp," Gordon speculated.

"That's possible," Constable McLeod said. "I'm checking every angle. This year I'm going to break this case. I'll search the camp and interview the lumberjacks. The woods around the camp are extremely difficult to search, even on horseback. That's why I brought the mustang. She was born in the wild and good at moving through rugged terrain. If anyone remembers anything, I'll be staying at the camp."

Not having to go to the camp, Gordon reached Gimley's place around two in the afternoon. He finished the chores in less than an hour and, as he walked back towards the house, he noticed a new Case manure spreader back of the barn.

Now, a manure spreader was not the most glamorous piece of equipment on a farm, but nonetheless it was the most envied. Without it, manure had to be loaded onto a wagon or stone boat and spread over the field with a pitchfork. Manure spreaders had only been on the market for a decade, and this one was a beauty!! It even had a tractor hitch conversion, and — it was already loaded with manure. Gordon remembered the fanfare when Albert purchased a tractor last spring. A tractor and a manure spreader! The temptation was too great. Besides, he reasoned, he would be helping his neighbors by spreading the load in the field before the tilling and seeding tomorrow. He brought the old Fordson Major steel-wheeled tractor around, hooked onto the manure spreader and headed for the field. He felt like a kid taking his dad's car for a spin. After pulling into the field, he stopped, engaged the axle and started spreading. The blades at the back of the machine whipped the manure evenly over the ground. It was truly remarkable.

But soon the spreader started making a grinding noise, and Gordon stopped to see what was caught in the blades. Using a stick, he poked the manure loose and discovered the obstruction was the sole of a boot — a tan work boot. And in the box of the spreader, a human hand protruded from the sleeve of a red plaid flannel shirt.

Constable George McLeod found all three bodies that summer. He brought in a two-bottom plow and turned up the oat field. The bodies were recovered from their resting place of the past year or two—under a crop of oats in summer and heavy snow in winter.

Quest for the God Particle

n the spring of 2008, above the rugged Chilean treescape, a giant awoke from a thousand-year sleep. With a vengeance he belched thick black smoke high into the night sky. Lightning arced and danced around the noxious plume that flowed from his cavernous mouth. He hissed, flicked out his fiery tongue and spewed brimstone down the mountainside incinerating everything in its wake. Mulciber rose with a terrifying rage.

At the opposite end of the earth, as dawn broke over rice fields in the peaceful Sichuan Basin of southwestern China, a restless Enceladus turns his weary sides and struggled to free himself from the crush of his mountainous grave. He shook the very foundations of a solid continent. In a great tectonic battle, the Indian plate rafted on molten asthenosphere and pushed up over the Eurasia plate, striking a northeast thrust along the Longmenshan fault bringing untold destruction to the rolling hills and alluvial plains of the Red Basin.

Meanwhile, along the border of Switzerland and France, between Lake Geneva and the Jura mountain range, deep in the bowels of the earth, subatomic particles hurl in opposite directions around a thirty-kilometer circular tunnel at temperatures colder than outer space. They gain energy with every lap until they collide at the speed of light. The quest for the unimaginable has begun. In the most spectacular research experiment ever undertaken on earth, scientists from around the globe search for the 'God Particle'.

Ten months later, Dr. Aaron Krause pushed his way through throngs of reporters on the steps of the United States District Court of Hawaii in Honolulu. With long straggly graying hair, mustache and beard, he epitomizes classic geek. After a life spent in the laboratory or behind mounds of scientific papers in his office in Switzerland, he is uncomfortable in a suit and indeed in this whole environment. Flashbulbs blind him, microphones jab at him and the questions keep coming.

"What do you think of Cern being slapped with the doomsday suit?"

"Do you think there is a chance the earth will disappear into a black hole?"

"Is LHC a doomsday machine?"

"Have you found the Higgs Boson?"

"Are the three explorers you sent down the wormhole still missing?"

The last question shook him and he looked around to see where it came from. No one knows about the time machine experiment.

Aaron bounded up the stairs and entered the building. He glanced at his watch. He only had five minutes. He scanned the display boards. 'Wagner vs. Cern & Fermilab', he read, 'Courtroom 6'.

"Aaron!" A tall man in a black suit and red tie waved him over.

"Warren Bailey?" Aaron asked.

"No, I'm David Meshenberg. I represent Fermilab, but we are working as a team." He directed Aaron towards a table at the front of the courtroom.

"All rise. The Right Honorable Justice Jackson presiding."

An attractive woman, in black robes, strode into the courtroom. Taking her place at the bench, she looked out over half-frame glasses. "I am to consider a petition from Walter Wagner, a former nuclear safety officer, to stop operations at the Cern laboratory in Switzerland and Fermi National Accelerator Laboratory in Illinois. The petitioners raise concerns that experiments at these two labs could have a catastrophic impact on earth. They contend that the Hadron Collider could create a black hole that could swallow up our planet."

"I feel the demise of the earth is greatly exaggerated, your Honor," Warren Bailey interceded, to laughter from the Cern table. "The Hadron Collider has been in full operation now for six months and the earth is still here."

"You will have your time to defend your client, Mr. Bailey. Your outburst is unacceptable. I will not tolerate ridicule in this courtroom. I intend to give this matter grave consideration."

"Yes, your Honor."

Addressing the petitioners, the judge said, "I am not a physicist, so I ask that you present your case in the simplest terms possible."

A round balding man rose. "George Cruz, your honor. I am counsel for the petitioner. If it please the court, your Honor, as I am not a physicist either, I would like to call Dr. Aaron Krause to the stand."

"Mr. Krause has been sworn," the bailiff affirmed.

"Very well, you may proceed Mr. Cruz."

The attorney cleared his throat. "Mr. Krause, could you state your affiliation with the laboratory in Switzerland?"

"I am a theoretical physicist and I have worked at Cern for fifteen years." Aaron felt his cell phone vibrating in the inside pocket of his sports jacket. He wished he could answer it but could only hope that they left a message. Have there been new developments with the time experiment?

"Dr. Krause, could you explain to the court what is going on at the Cern laboratory and what is hoped to be accomplished by these experiments?"

"You want me to explain particle physics in simple terms?

"You don't need to explain particle physics, Dr. Krause, just what is going on in your laboratory."

"The LHC is designed to fire a stream of subatomic particles into each other at near the speed of light. When they collide, these protons will be smashed into tiny fireballs of primordial energy much like what existed when the universe was less than a trillionth of a second old. In simple terms we are trying to recreate the big bang."

The judge interrupted, "By LHC, are you referring to the Large Hadron Collider?"

Aaron's eyes lit up. "Correct," he said. "The beams of subatomic particles that collide with each other are called hadrons and the collider is large in every possible way. It cost eight billion dollars to build, uses fourteen trillion electron volts of energy and takes 128 tons of liquid helium to cool the magnets that propel the particles around their track. Thousands of top physicists around the world are involved in the experiment, and it will take three million DVDs to hold the data we collect each year."

The judge smiled at Aaron's child-like enthusiastic response. "Thank you Dr. Krause. That certainly puts it in perspective. Please continue."

"The accelerator will take physics into a whole new realm of energy and time that that we can only philosophize about today." Aaron's voice was still filled with enthusiasm. "It will take us back to a time when the universe was evolving from a primordial state of potential energy into the forces and matter that we see today. What we learn from it will change our whole concept of the cosmos and our position in it. It will answer the questions that perplexed Einstein. Are there extra dimensions of space out there that haven't yet been detected? What is dark matter? But our ultimate goal is the search for the Higgs Boson, the mysterious particle that we think gives other particles mass."

"So would you say you are looking for the Force? Sort of the way Jedi Knight in Star Wars is the carrier of the force?" the counselor asked.

"Yes, the fifth force is the Higgs field. For years physicists have thought that a fifth force exists. I think the creators of Star Wars took the theory that a fifth force exists and personified it in the Jedi Knight. We expect to get data from the LHC that will prove that it exists. Most physicists believe there must be a Higgs field that permeates space and interacts with everything living and inert. The Higgs boson is the carrier particle of the Higgs field. It is the missing piece of the puzzle and the cornerstone of particle physics, but no one has ever found it. Now, we are on the brink of doing just that."

"Well, let the force be with you," the attorney said to laughter from the Wagner table.

"Order," the judge tapped her gavel. "Try not to be too flippant in my courtroom, Mr. Cruz."

"Yes, Your Honor," Cruz responded and then turned his attention back to the witness. "Now tell me, Dr. Krause, this Higgs Boson that you talk about, is it sometimes called the God Particle?"

"Yes, but that term is used mostly by the media. It isn't used by scientists."

The lawyer walked back to his table and consulted with a member of his team, then whirled back to the witness and asked, "Are you familiar with the term black holes?"

"Yes, of course."

"Would you agree that they are the most fearsome objects in the universe? They swallow and destroy everything that crosses their path?"

"They have been considered in that light, but…"

"Just yes or no."

"Yes, you could say that."

"In your opinion could the experiments taking place at Cern produce black holes?"

"There are some physicists that think microscopic black holes could be produced by the collisions but if there were any they would be too small to generate enough gravitational force to pull in surrounding matter. If it were possible for the LHC to produce black holes, then the cosmic rays from the sun would already have produced a lot more than Cern could ever hope to. Collisions provided by Nature over billions of years have not harmed the Earth, so I think it would be safe to say there is no reason to worry about black holes."

"But some of your contemporaries predict that millions of black holes might persist long enough to be captured by earth's gravity and accumulate in the earth's core where they could coalesce into a compact mass. That mass would draw in other matter and eventually cause the earth to collapse in on itself."

"That's pure science fiction," Aaron scoffed. "Any black holes would only exist for a fleeting moment. Then all their matter would evaporate into energy and they would disappear."

The attorney paced the floor before coming back to stand directly in front of the witness box. "But would you have to admit that you are sailing into uncharted waters? That anytime a scientist conducts an experiment he runs the chance of finding something he had never expected or indeed could never even have dreamt of? Could something go wrong with the experiment—maybe a faulty calculation or a faulty assumption? Is this experiment not human arrogance and recklessness at its finest? Or do you consider particle physicists to be infallible, Dr. Krause?"

Before Aaron could answer, the judge interrupted. "My mind is whirling and it's long past my lunch hour. I think we will adjourn here for the day and resume tomorrow morning at nine."

George Cruz felt a wave of disappointment. He had spent the morning warming up to this moment. He was poised and ready to hit the witness with some really stinging questions. "I haven't finished with this witness yet, Your Honor. I haven't touched on magnetic monopoles or strangelets or traversable wormholes. If it would please the court I could wrap it up in a half hour to forty-five minutes."

"I think not, Mr. Cruz. I need the rest of the day to digest what has been said so far. Both sides have presented compelling arguments. I need time to weigh the statements. We will resume tomorrow morning." She brought the gavel down, ending the day's session.

❖

Meanwhile
Sixty-six Million Years Back in Time

The sun gleamed off of the calm waters of the Cretaceous Inner Sea. Rebecca stared in disbelief. It all happened so fast. She felt as though she had lost time somewhere along the way. It was like the feeling one gets when waking from an anesthetic induced sleep. The last thing she remembered was waiting with her two traveling buddies in the time-machine cabinet. Their departure was to be delayed for another hour or so while technicians worked out a glitch. But here she stood. And it was everything she could ever have imagined. A rush of adrenaline and a complete sense of tranquility came over her at the same instance.

"Becky!" Sunitha and Garret were walking down the sandy beach towards her. "Wow, can you believe this place?" Garret beamed. "Does anyone have any idea where we are exactly?"

Rebecca shielded her eyes with her hand and looked up at the sun. "It looks like its high noon by the position of the sun. And by the angle of the sun I would guess it is either spring or late fall in the far north."

"Look at the flowers on the trees in the swamp behind us. They almost look like magnolia blossoms. It's probably spring," Sunitha added. "We'll be able to get a better feel for our location when the stars come out."

"Does anyone else sense something so phenomenally different about this place?" Garret asked. "I mean aside from the fact that we are standing on the fucking shores of the Inner Cretaceous Seaway, sixty-six million years back in time? The scenery could be any remote tropical shoreline in modern times. The trees and grass don't look too alien. The sun is in the sky and the water is blue. But there is something very weird. I can't put my finger on it."

"The silence!" the two young women exclaimed in unison. "It's deafening! Even with the wind rustling though the tall grasses and the water lapping on the shoreline, the silence is massive. It feels as though our voices are being swallowed up into a huge void."

"Speaking of silence, I guess we should let Cern know we've arrived safely," Garret said. "Sunny, do you have the transmitter?"

Sunitha reached in the bag strapped around her waist and pulled out a video camera. "I'm on it," she said. "I can just see the expression on their faces when they see what I'm about to send them. Smile," she said as she began to roll the video. She scanned the ocean and her friends on the beach and then shot video as she walked through the tall grass and into the lush vegetation. "Hey! Come over here and see this," she exclaimed. "Bees—there are bees in the magnolia flowers so big they're the size of humming birds. Were there insects back then?"

"Of course there were. Insects co-evolved with flowering plants," Garret said as he surveyed the forested swampland. "A lot of palms and cyclads and a few conifers and what is that flowering shrub over there?" he asked. "It looks like it might be a fruit tree of some sort—maybe a fig. From the look of the lush vegetation it shouldn't be hard to find enough food to keep us going."

"Look at the ant hill," Sunitha exclaimed. "And the butterflies. I expected a huge diversity of dinosaurs not this abundant insect life. Ouch!" she said slapping her arm. "Something just bit me."

"I've been swatting something that looks like wasps since I came into the swamp. But we had better get busy preparing for our first night under the stars. I'll gather some shellfish for supper. Becky could you find some dry firewood? What do you say we build a fire on the beach and gather some ferns or big leaves to sleep on? Maybe we could even build some kind of a makeshift shelter."

Rebecca put her hand up to hush him. She had the eerie sense that they were being watched and was searching the vegetation for a pair of eyes. She happened to glance up and her gaze passed across the motionless head of a dinosaur above the treetops looking directly down at her. She froze. "Hey guys," she said steadily. "Don't scream, just look up above the conifer to the right of the tulip tree."

"Oh my Gawd!" the two exclaimed. Sunitha aimed the video at the large creature looking down at them. "It looks like a real live Tyrannosaurus Rex," she said excitedly.

"We may not be eating supper tonight. We may be supper," Garret said. "We would be easy prey for a T. Rex. As a matter of fact we would just be one bite for him—just a mid-afternoon snack."

"Or her," Sunitha cut in. "I see two baby dinosaurs playing under the canopy near her. She doesn't look like she's stalking us. Maybe she's just curious or watching out for her young."

"We had better build a big bonfire," Garret said. "Hopefully she will be afraid of fire. Sunny, you keep and eye on Momma there. I'll gather some wood and Becky can start a fire in a clump of grass right away."

Once the bonfire was blazing the gigantic mother could be seen, and indeed felt, moving her brood farther into the swamp-forest.

Later that afternoon the three hungry explorers sat around the fire on the seashore and roasted their supper. Garret had gathered clams and oysters and some crab-like marine life. There was even something for dessert that resembled planes or figs that Rebecca had plucked from the trees in the swamp. A large fruit from a palm tree, that resembled a coconut, lay on the sand ready to be broken into. "Have you ever seen shell fish this big before?" Garret asked. "And when I was gathering food I saw a gigantic ray and a huge turtle like nothing I've ever seen before. Texas has nothing on this place."

A large bird appeared in the sky and dove down into the sea in front of them. The sight was an optical anomaly totally alien to the three onlookers. It was as though they were looking at a multiple exposure picture. The bird caused a large splash as it descended below the surface of the water. The resulting concentric waves looked normal but when the bird rose from the waters carrying its prey, twisting and writhing between its teeth, the peculiar optics reoccurred. The three sat mesmerized. "W-w-hat?" Sunitha uttered. "Huh?" Garret asked. "Did everyone see what I just did?" Rebecca asked. "I thought my eyes were playing tricks on me. What could cause that?"

"We're in a different dimension," Garret exclaimed. "I went to a physics lecture once on alternative dimensions. The speaker was describing how we would visualize something in another dimension. She said someone in a 3-dimensional world, who could only see in 2-dimension, would see a series of slices of the object, much in the way a CAT Scan takes pictures. Then they would have to reconstruct the images by stacking them on top of one another to get a 3-dimensional image. Someone who can only visualize in 3-dimension but sees something in the fifth dimension, would visualize the object as a series of 3-dimensional objects stacked on top of one another. I think that is what we were seeing. Time is the fourth dimension and somehow when we were transported back in time we traversed across another dimensional field."

"So what does that mean?" Sunitha asked. "Are we still able to communicate with Cern? I've been having a problem transmitting the pictures. I thought that maybe I just had to wait a while. Could the fact that we are in a different dimension of space affect transmission?"

"I can't tell you," Garret replied. "We're breaking new ground here. Scientists have long thought there were extra dimensions but no one has ever demonstrated their existence. Scientists just know that the only way they can explain the weakness of the gravity particle compared to the other forces is that gravity bubbles out of our three dimensional space and into other dimensions. As a matter of fact, scientists think there are more than five dimensions. They think there may be as many as twelve."

"I'm not in the mood for a physics lecture right now Garret," Rebecca broke in. "I'm scared. Suppose we are cut off from 2008 all together? This is an exciting place to visit but I don't want to stay here for the rest of my life."

Garret laughed. "That's a bit of a trite expression."

"It's not funny," Rebecca snapped. "This was supposed to be a three-month expedition. What if they can never find us?" Then she brightened with renewed hope. "They'll figure it out at Cern. They must be frantic that they haven't heard from us by now. And they have the brains and the manpower to figure it out."

"I hope you're right," Sunitha said. "My arm is swelling up like a watermelon and I don't feel too well. I think I have a bit of a fever." Her two friends hurried over to her side.

Sunitha's face was moist and flushed. "My God, you really are having a bad reaction to the wasp sting," Rebecca said. "Does anyone have any idea what to do? Look at her ankles! They're swollen up too."

"I know that people use plantain to soothe bug bites. You just chew the leaves and then put them on the bite, but I don't know if we could find any plant here with the same medicinal properties," Garret said. "We could try making poultices of different leaves but there is always the possibility that Sunny could have an allergic reaction to the plants. I don't understand why Sunny is having such a severe reaction and all we had was the normal itchiness."

"It's probably because she is Sri Lankan and her immune system would have evolved differently from ours," Rebecca said. "And maybe since we grew up in the American midwest, our immune system was exposed to a descendent of these prehistoric insects. Garret, could you dip your T-shirt into the water and bring it to me. I'm going to try to bring her fever down. See if you can get some fluid out of that coconut or what ever it is. We don't want her to get dehydrated."

In their efforts to tend to Sunitha they forgot about their other problems and by nightfall they fell into an exhausted sleep only to be abruptly awakened by a large fireball streaking across the night sky."I hope that's not the asteroid that wiped out the dinosaurs," Garret said pessimistically.

To be continued…

Dance with a Spanish Lady

An excerpt from *The Devil's Ruse*

Captain Parker poised his scalpel poised over the young corpse and made an incision down the center of the chest. Wresting the ribcage open, he exposed the chest cavity. What they saw was shocking.

A nurse recorded as the army pathologist, dictated. "September 18, 1918. Private Bruce Jones: Chest cavity filled with fluid, lungs blue and swollen. Estimate three hundred milliliters of clear fluid in the chest cavity." Parker reached into the cavity and cut out the left lung. A bloody froth exuded from the insubstantial tissue. "The lungs are distended by an exudation of fluid into the interalveolar walls and by a large emphysematous space due to their rupture. The surface of the lung is mottled with numerous hemorrhages. The fissures range in size from a pinprick to two centimeters in diameter. The bronchi and bronchioles are filled with serous fluid and show necrosis and exfoliation of their epithelium. Death appears to be due to asphyxiation. His lungs were rendered useless."

Turning to Nicholas, Parker remarked, "This is a most unusual pathological picture. There is a complete absence of pneumonias of ordinary bacterial origin. What do you make of it?"

"Bizarre beyond belief!" Nicholas said. "Healthy men dropping dead on the spot! This epidemic ravages swifter and is more pervasive than the bubonic plague."

"It's the most vicious form of pneumonia I've ever encountered," added Parker. "I've prepared some swabs of the fluid for you to culture. I would be interested to know is there is some type of secondary microorganism that we haven't seen before," He cut off lung sections and dropped them into a vial of formaldehyde. "Could you forward some of the samples to Washington, Nick?"

Two more cadavers presented much the same autopsy features. Both had been healthy, young men who were struck down suddenly. One had presented to sickbay on the morning of September 13th. He ran a high fever and was delirious. The next day his skin turned black. Three days later, his temperature dropped dramatically below normal, and he died. The other soldier became ill on September 16th. He presented to sickbay, at 18:00 hours, feeling achy and feverish and in a state of delirium. His feet had turned black. He died during the night.

When the autopsies were finished, Captain Parker wiped the sweat from his forehead, and said, "I need some fresh air."

Out in the sunshine, James Parker looked haggard. He was a portly man of about forty, but stress lines etched deep into his face. "The Surgeon General is sending William Henry Welch to Camp Devens tomorrow to try to figure out what is going on," he said.

"I heard," Nicholas replied. "Rufus Cole from the Institute, Colonel Victor Vaughan and Simeon Walbach from Harvard will be joining him—a team of the who's who in infectious diseases. It's rumored that Gorgas, himself, might even attend."

"We all feared that the overcrowding in the camps would be a problem, but never imagined anything of this magnitude," Parker commented. "The overcrowding was bad enough before General Foch was appointed Supreme Commander of the Allies on the Western Front. General Pershing only figured on sending a few hundred thousand American soldiers to Europe, but General Foch called for millions." The exhausted pathologist shook his head wearily. "Well, this contagion is certainly wrecking havoc with those plans; many draft orders have had to be cancelled."

Afternoon waned, and the sun's fading light cast shadows on the sea of confusion engulfing the hospital entrance. A stream of men —faces blue and in bloodstained drab olive— crowded in.

"They flood in continuously," Parker said. "And in the morning the dead are stacked about the morgue like cordwood. The thing that tires me the most is that we don't know what to do. With all our great modern day medical achievements, we can't touch it. The medical profession stands with head bowed."

Nicholas lifted his bicycle out of the rack. "I have to get to Upton Station before the last train leaves for New York City. I'll ring you with the lab results."

Riding westward, Nicholas tried to rid his mind of the horrors of the day. The treeless area that had been carved out of the woods just a year ago, to make way for Upton Army Training Camp, spread out before him. A full moon appeared in the early evening sky as dusk fell. Feeling fatigued and clammy, Nicholas hoped the cool evening breeze and the solitude of the four-mile ride to the train station would refresh him. Ominous clouds loomed on the western horizon, and moonlight illuminated the road that stretched to the edge

of the forest. Nicholas escaped into the beautiful phrases of
The Highwayman.

The moon was a ghostly gallon tossed upon cloudy seas
The road was a ribbon of moonlight, over the purple moor

The cold breeze felt good on his exposed skin, but he
soon took a chill and drew his cape close about him. In the
woods, the road became darker, and he lit the headlamp. The
underbellies of aspen leaves glistened in the moonlight and
brought the lyrics of Alfred Noyes flooding back.

The wind was a torrent of darkness among the gusty trees.

Peddling harder, sweat poured down his back. He unbuttoned his cape and threw it off his neck. His body ached, his
eyes burned, and his nose ran. A heavy weariness descended
on him, and he started coughing—a cough so all consuming
that he lost control of his bicycle and slid on the dirt road.
Tasting salt in his mouth, he thought, "It must be blood! My
nose must be bleeding." He fumbled for his handkerchief and
held it to his nose tilting his face upwards. A bright light lit
up the night, and thunder rumbled. The skies opened and
torrential rains washed his burning face. His body shivered.
For a brief moment, he felt lucid again. The station could
only be half an hour's ride. He struggled to right his bicycle.
"Bess will be waiting and watching for me," he thought, "I
promised to return by midnight." He pressed on, coughing
uncontrollably. "But I shouldn't be going home to carry this
sickness to my family! I should turn around and head back
to the camp hospital. But which way am I headed? Where
am I? What am I doing here?" Standing on the edge of the

road, he tried to focus and then collapsed on the grass. He
felt excruciating pain behind his eyes, and heard the death
rattle in his chest. Between each coughing attack, he gasped
desperately for air —loud, hoarse and rapid. Frothy fluid
caked his chin and neck.

They shot him down on the highway
Down like a dog on the highway
And he lay in his blood on the highway…

The words resonated in the recesses of his mind. He felt
his soul move out of his body and hover. An intense peace
befell him. Now he looked down and marveled at the stature
of the body he had just left. Forty-two years he had lived in
that body, and, strangely, he had never realized how tall and
lanky it was. One leg extended straight out behind, and
the other knee was bent; his cape swept out behind him as
though the wind were blowing it away from him. His silhouette looked like he was running, and reminded him of
Ichabod Crane!

Bells clanged in the distance. Lights of an ambulance
picked up the bicycle lying on the road. Attendants jumped
out and scurried about. At that moment, his soul returned
to his body, and he felt the full impact of his agony again.
Someone wiped blood from his face and placed a plug in his
nose. An engine started. The ambulance bounced over the
dirt road. "I must have missed something," he thought. "I
must be on the way to the hospital, but I don't remember
being lifted into the car. No, that's not it. I am being taken
out of the car. I must have missed something again." When
he opened his eyes, the sun was high in the sky and he lay on
a cot in an open-air hospital tent.

"He's stirring," Nicholas heard a female voice say. Addressing him, she said, "I think the rain saved your life. The cool water brought your temperature down."

The Spanish Lady had danced her fury, but Nicholas survived.

The Bubble

An excerpt from *The Devil's Ruse*

My grandfather never talked about the Great War or the influenza pandemic of 1918. It was as though those four years were a forgotten part of his memory, locked away somewhere in the hidden recesses of his brain. He never talked about it, that is, until towards the latter years of his life. Then he talked a lot about the ugliness of the war and the catastrophic pestilence that brought it to an end. He told the stories with such clarity and precision that they could have happened yesterday. It was as if he had stored the memories away with the care that one might store forbidden love letters, meticulously tying them up in a bundle and hiding them away in a shoebox in the attic. Those memories had not been worn over the years with retelling; so precious they were to him that not one detail had been altered or omitted. The story he recounted the most was the one about 'the bubble'. It took place the day my grandmother died. This is his story.

My grandfather, Dr. Nicholas Wareing, was a bacteriologist, and during the war years he worked in an infectious disease laboratory at the Rockefeller Institute in New York City. His 'bubble' story began one Sunday afternoon, late in September of 1918. He and his assistant, Garrison, were alone in their laboratory that day, working feverishly to uncover the cause of the pandemic that gripped the world. The radio in the laboratory blared out the latest news broadcast.

"The pandemic wreaks havoc with the war machine," the commentator proclaimed. "The Provost Marshall General of the United States Army cancelled a draft call of 142,000 men this morning. The recruits are all sick or quarantined and training has come to a standstill. Influenza also ravages wartime industry. Arsenal factories and ship building yards have ground to a halt."

The news ended and the evangelist, Billy Sunday, began broadcasting live from his home in Chicago.

"I guess now that all public gatherings are forbidden, the Reverend has to spread his message of salvation over the radio waves," Nicholas said.

Sunday's voice boomed over the airways. "Influenza is all a big German plot," he declared, and Nicholas could just picture him standing in front of the microphone with an open Bible in his outstretched hand. "It started over there in Spain where the Germans scattered all those germs around." His voice was full of passion, and it intensified as he spoke. "There is nothing short of hell the Prussians won't stoop to. Damn their hides! This is not an earthly disease we have among us. It is the Devil's 'flu, and sin has caused it.

Yes, nothing short of sin has brought this evil pestilence down upon us, and nothing short of prayer can cure it. I'm calling on all Americans in this grand land of ours to get down on their knees and pray down this epidemic."

Garrison reached over Nicholas and switched the radio off in disgust. "Pray down the epidemic! Devil's flu! I can just picture the Germans scattering germs around like they were seeding a field or something. What utter religious nonsense." Garrison said.

"Sunday's not the only one that is spreading that ridiculous conjecture," Nicholas replied. "Just the other day the

New York Post proclaimed that all epidemics were nature's way of punishing us. The *New York Post*, grant you! And then, there's the eminent Lieutenant Colonel Philip Doane, the head of Health and Sanitation for the Army Emergency Fleet Corps. He's supporting this nonsense. And not just privately. He was quoted on the front page of last Saturday's *Philadelphia Inquirer*."

"I suppose people are so scared they have to make sense of the whole thing anyway they can."

"God knows the scientific and medical professions can't come up with a plausible explanation for where it came from so people have to grasp at straws," Nicholas said. "You know, I was talking to Philip Doane last week and he had me wondering whether it could have been biological warfare."

"You? I never would have guessed it."

"There could be some truth to the reports that a camou-flaged U-boat crept into Boston Harbor at night and released the germs," Nicholas said. "The Germans have always excelled in the field of bacteriology."

"You need some rest Nick. You've been here since five this morning. Why don't you go home? I can finish up here."

It was only four o'clock but Nicholas decided to take Garrison up on his offer. He was frustrated by the confusing and conflicting lab results they were getting. He had not been able to culture anything that looked like the bacillus that was thought to have caused the pandemic. He would take a break now and continue again tomorrow morning when he was fresh.

"Garrison, I'm going to do just that. I'm going home now." Nicholas pulled on his jacket. "I'll see you in the morning."

Nicholas decided to stop in town on the way home. The grocer, old Mr. Harbinger, had promised to put aside some oranges for him, and he needed to stop at the Chemist Shop for some elixir and camphor. So he took the dirt road that headed south from Harris Corner into town. Ambulances and trucks rattled passed him on their way to pick up the sick and the dead.

The streets of the normally bustling town were empty. Most of the businesses were closed. Some had their windows boarded up to prevent looting. As Nicholas entered the deserted main street, an eerie feeling of foreboding came over him. A screen door banged against the wall of a building in the wind. A poster on a telephone pole had partially torn loose and was flapping in the wind. It read:

WEAR A MASK AND SAVE YOUR LIFE
OBEY THE LAWS AND WEAR THE GUAZE
PROTECT YOUR JAWS FROM SEPTIC PAWS

The sign was a reminder that the town had issued an ultimatum that no one was allowed in a public place without a mask. The sign had been tacked over a recruitment poster. Uncle Sam looked out over the sign. He wore his patriotic top hat but his finger that had pointed directly at the reader and the words *I Want YOU for the US Army* were hidden. The image said it all. The influenza pandemic had eclipsed the Great War.

Nicholas pulled his mask on as he entered the main street of the town. A lone man wearing the gauze was spraying the street with disinfectant. Suddenly sounds of laughter and merriment broke the ethereal stillness. Three inebriated men staggered out of a tavern. They were singing and shouting and waving their bottles of gin around. *Everything closes down except the taverns*! Nicholas thought. *Taverns must be considered to be as essential as the grocery stores or the chemist shops.* Jake, the undertaker, was talking to someone on the sidewalk outside his funeral home. The three drunken men ostentatiously gave him a wide berth. "I don't like the way he's looking at us," the burly one laughed. "He looks like he's trying to drum up more business," the skinny one said.

That looks like Dan Hemple, the schoolteacher, Nicholas thought. After looking closer at the men, Nicholas realized he recognized all three. One worked over in the lumber mill and the other he had seen from time to time at the Methodist church.

Noticing Nicholas, Dan shouted, "Hey, there's the good professor. Doesn't he just look like the typical professor, boys? Yup, a real Dr. Jeckle. I wonder what secret sinister experiments he does in his labs every day." Dan's speech was slurred. He crossed the street and approached Nicholas, all the time waving the bottle around with one arm. "Nicholas, my friend, come and join us. We're just going to catch the game on the radio down at McGinty's."

"Thanks, Dan, but I'm anxious to get home. My wife and girls weren't feeling well when I left this morning."

"Jeez, Professor, you're no fun at all." Dan's two cohorts had continued on down the street without him. "Hey, wait for me you two wankers," Dan shouted after them. "I thought it was one for all and all for one. We're supposed to be the three musketeers remember?" Nicholas watched as they meandered happily down the street and into the next open bar.

Nicholas picked up the items at the Chemist Shop and headed towards the grocery store. On the street outside Harbinger's Grocery stood a red wagon with pinewood sides three panels high. Two young boys were coming out of the store carrying bags of groceries. One boy, about eight years old, was struggling with a sack of flour. The boys were dressed in their Boy Scout uniforms and around their necks hung camphor bags.

Everywhere you go, camphor bags and the smell of camphor, Nicholas thought. *I am so sick of the smell of camphor.*

"Hi Dr. Wareing," they said.

"Hi boys," Nicholas replied with a look of amusement at the large load one youngster was carrying. "Need some help?"

"No, I can manage," the youngster said proudly as he practically fell into the wagon with the flour.

"Getting groceries for your Mom?" Nicholas asked.

"Nope, we're taking this load over to the Richardson's. This is our last delivery. We had three this afternoon."

"I knew you delivered food baskets to the quarantined but I didn't know you got groceries for them too."

"Yep," they both answered excitedly. "Anybody needs groceries they put a note in a milk bottle outside their door," said one.

"Mr. Harbinger fills the order and puts it on their bill," said the other.

"You're really doing an excellent service to the community, boys." Nicholas watched with a feeling of warmth as the two set out pulling the heavily laden wagon down the street.

"Got your oranges," Harold Harbinger called as Nicholas entered the store.

"Thanks Harold," Nicholas said. "It seems like there is a smell of sulfur burning in here."

"Oh, yes. My wife makes me sprinkle sulfur over the wood in the stove every day. She tells me to lean over the fire and inhale the fumes every so often. It's supposed to fumigate me.

"How is your wife?"

"Oh, she's doing all right. She wishes she was able to go and help at the hospitals but it's her knees, you know. She can't get around as well as she would like to. That's why she boils up the soups all day. She makes the most beautiful vegetable and meat soups and has them in thermos flasks for the boys to pick up every morning. I think it's helped a lot of people survive. You really have to admire the kids. They work hard all day and they're so eager. The women can cook the food but without the kids to distribute it we couldn't get supplies out to nearly so many of the quarantined. The kids have probably saved many lives. If the empty containers are not on the doorstep the next day, the kids know there is something wrong, and we send for an ambulance."

Nicholas thanked Harold for the oranges, and, taking his coveted citrus with him, he left the store and headed home.

As he passed the Milton place, Martha Milton was by the side of the road getting mail out of the mailbox. She wore a yellow dress with lace and ruffles at the neck.

"Mighty fine dress, Martha," Nicholas said.

"Oh! Dr. Wareing! I haven't seen you in quite some time. I have the coffeepot on and a freshly baked apple pie. Can you come in for a few minutes?"

Nicholas was feeling the pangs of hunger, and he was also starved for some semblance of normality. This seemed it. "Why, yes. That is a nice idea." For the moment, he threw all concerns and responsibility to the wayside and indulged himself in this small break. Martha was pleased and chatted excitedly as she led the way through the picket gate and up the path to the cottage. She stopped to pick some daisies that were still growing wild in the ditch at the sides of the gates even after the light frost of a few nights ago. "Daisies are my favorite flower," she said. "They always remind me of purity and simplicity."

William Milton appeared in the doorway. He looked especially relaxed and happy. "Hi Nick. It's great the see you again. Come in. Come in. Polly put the kettle on and we'll all have tea," he rattled off the nursery rhyme with great merriment.

This is starting to spook me, Nicholas thought. *It's as though they are oblivious to the fact that we are living in the middle of hell. Don't they hear the death trucks rumbling by? Don't they read the papers or hear the news?* But at the same time this escape from reality was such a welcome relief that Nicholas decided to savor the moment.

"You're looking especially fit this afternoon, William. I can't stay long but I would welcome a hot cup of coffee and a slice of that great apple pie that Martha makes."

William held the door open and ushered Nicholas in with a great flourish. The front door opened into a modest sized room that served as the kitchen and living room combined. The kitchen table stood by the window in one corner of the room as usual but today it was adorned with a crocheted tablecloth. The wood stove stood against the opposite wall and in the corner was a crude wood box. Between the stove and the wood box, against a backdrop of faded yellow plasterboard, stood an elegant Ethan Allen French Provincial high-winged-back-chair in green and blue paisley-patterned upholstery. Its elegant claw-foot legs stood on the worn black and white checkered linoleum floor. Martha took a vase from the cupboard, placed the daisies in it and ceremoniously placed the arrangement in the center of the table.

"Come over here and see my new gramophone, Nick." William lifted the lid and placed a record on the turnstile and wound the crank on the side. Strains of a piano rendition of *Beautiful Ohio* filled the small room. Martha was setting out her best china and displayed her shiny new sterling silver coffeepot.

"My, but this is all very nice," Nicholas said.

William seemed to be in a trance listening to the music and, without looking at Nicholas he said, "Did you know that Mary Earl is not really Mary Earl. He's really Robert King. And he lives right here in New York City. Mary Earl is just his pen name. But he sure did compose one of the most beautiful waltzes this world has ever known. Beautiful lyrics too. You need to listen to the lyrics, Nick." William stood silently swaying to the music and his lips moved as he silently sang along with the artist. When the record finished, he turned back to the gramophone to make another selection. "Do you like Scott Joplin, Nick? I've got *The Entertainer*. I've also got *Alexander's Ragtime Band*." Nicholas watched as William proudly sorted through his collection of music. "I have quite a collection of ragtime. Nathan likes ragtime. It's his favorite music."

Cold shivers ran up Nicholas's spine. *Nathan likes ragtime? Likes? Present tense?* Harold Harbinger's words echoed in his mind. "Martha and William Milton's only son, Nathan, was wounded at Flanders. He was treated in a field hospital in Belgium before being transferred to a military hospital in France where he had both legs amputated. He was then sent home but died during the voyage." Then the blood in Nicholas's veins froze solid when he remembered Harold's words a few days later. "There was no funeral service," he had said. "The Miltons are said to have buried their son on their property. Wanted to keep him safely close at home with them, they said."

Through the fog of his fright Nicholas could hear William's calm pleasant voice. "All my life I've dreamed of having a gramophone this beautiful. I could sit and listen to this music all day. Isn't she just the most beautiful machine you've ever seen?"

Nicholas tried to compose himself and moved towards the gramophone to examine it. "It is indeed the most beautiful gramophone I think I've ever seen, William," Nicholas said. He opened the door to the storage cabinet below the turnstile inspecting the machine. "Mahogany floor cabinet model! I've never seen one like it."

"It's made by Berliner. A real work of beauty. Martha and I saw it in Eaton's and decided we just had to have it, so we cashed some liberty bonds and brought it home with us. Best move I've ever made. What good is a liberty bond to anyone anyway? Can't get any music out of a liberty bond. Can't eat it. Can't even get pleasure out of looking at it."

Nicholas was shaken by William and Martha's complete removal from reality but for the moment, in this room, with the crocheted tablecloth, the music, the freshly brewed coffee poured from a silver coffee pot, he escaped the world for a few happy minutes. No smell of camphor permeated the room. The interminable racket of the trucks carrying the dead could not be heard over the beautiful piano music coming from the handsome gramophone. The cottage was a haven from all the pain and worry. He drank his coffee and they talked about things that could have you believe that there was some sense in the world and everything outside these cottage walls was just a bad nightmare. The whole past four years never existed. It couldn't be happening. Nothing this horrific could be real.

They discussed how Cecil B. DeMille had discovered the beautiful and talented Leatrice Joy. They marveled at Einstein's lecture on gravitational waves and about Ruth's incredible string of scoreless innings and how it had ended last week when the Cubs tied up the World Series in the 8ᵗʰ, and how Ruth batted in two runs on a triple in the 4ᵗʰ.

Warm thoughts coursed through Nicholas. "You know", he said, "I think it is indeed the best of times. Will anyone ever live that can exceed The Babe? Will there ever be anyone more beautiful and talented than Leatrice Joy, any scientist greater than Einstein, any author more talented thanGeorge Bernard Shaw? This is a good time to be alive. Great things are happening. Great people are alive." Nicholas wished that this moment would never end and that he would never have to leave this cottage room. Things made sense within these walls; beyond them lay madness. At length, he forced himself to rise.

"Oh dear. I lost track of time. I must be going."

William pulled out a shiny new gold watch from his pocket, and proudly looked at it. "It's almost five thirty," he said.

Nicholas took his leave, thanked his hosts and headed down the dirt road towards home. Five minutes before he reached his lane, an ambulance, bells tinkling, overtook him leaving him in a cloud of dust. When he turned the corner onto his side street, Nicholas could see that the ambulance was parked in front of his house. They had just loaded someone into it and were preparing to leave. Panic-stricken, he flung the bike to the ground and rushed to the departing ambulance. Oranges rolled out onto the street.

My grandmother died that day and my grandfather was not at her side; a regret he carried to his grave. He had been drinking coffee in the 'bubble', as he called it, at the time of her passing.

But my grandfather never ended the story with details of the loss of his beloved wife. That he kept to himself. Instead, he always concluded his story with his theory about the roaring twenties.

"It is no coincidence that the roaring twenties followed short on the heels of the Great War and the great influenza pandemic," he would say. "The whole world wrapped itself in a cocoon after those terrible times. The French called it the 'années folles', or the crazy years. Jazz music blossomed, the flapper redefined womanhood and an atmosphere of amusement, fun and lightness prevailed in defiance of the horrors of the past decade. There is a threshold of misery that the human spirit can bear," he would say. "When that threshold is exceeded, people wall themselves off from the outside world and exist in the security of their bubble."

Out of the Garden

A fictional story based on accounts in the Apocrypha,
the Pseudepigrapha and other Hebrew texts

Ana walked with her head down listening to the rhythm of her blistered feet on the desert sand. Her family was one of many moving sheep and goats eastward to better grazing land in Qumran. They had persevered through three years of drought, but this year dust storms and fires ravaged the Upper Nile Valley forcing them from their lands.

A dull ache radiated across her lower back, and Ana paused to rest. Pulling the scarf from her nose, she reached under her cloak and rested one hand on her belly. Through the layers of clothing that held her secret, she felt the baby kick.

Dust hung heavy beneath the lingering afternoon sun. Ana waited for the pain to subside, and her absent gaze rested on something off in the distance. As the image came into focus, her heart gladdened. Jericho! She had heard amazing stories about this city—about how you could smell its fragrance from anywhere in the Jordon Rift Valley—a welcome thought. Ana's nostrils had been filled with the scent of desert dust for too long.

Ana's father walked up behind her. He too had stopped to savor the first sight of the legendary city. "This city has been here since the beginning of time," he mused. "It's built on the top of a great mound that rises from the desert basin."

He leaned closer to his daughter and said, "When we get nearer, you will be able to see a tower rising above the city's walls. Just like our Lion in Giza, their tower aligns with the rising solstice sun."

Ana and her father started walking again.

"Tell me about the fragrance," Ana said.

"You're in for a amazing experience," her father said. "Jericho has a splendid garden with palm orchards and all manner of fragrant fruit trees. Many springs well up from the ground inside its walls and irrigate the Garden."

Ana asked, "Will we live there?"

"That would be wonderful, but I think not," her father replied. "The people of Jericho are very affluent. Some call them luminaries. They come from the continent to the north of the Great Crystal Sea and speak a language that is foreign to us. They wear fine clothes of silk and linen and make their own honey,"

"So why can't we live there?"

"Because they built a high wall around the city to keep nomads like us out—two walls in fact, one inside the other and both three times as high as you. And outside those walls is a very wide moat."

"Do they ever come out of the city?"

Yes, they come in and out. There are four gates in the outer wall, one facing each direction. The only way to get into the city is through one of the gates, and they're heavily guarded. We will camp outside the city. The water from the springs in the city flows out of the Garden and provides fresh drinking water for us and lush grasslands for our herds."

It was late day when Ana's family arrived at Jericho, and they set up camp in the shadow of the mountains.

The land surrounding the city was more than Ana could ever have imagined. Trees grew around fresh water lakes in the alluvial basin, and ducks swam lazily on the rivers and reed beds, basking in the last crimson rays of day.

As night fell over the valley, thunderclouds rolled in and shrouded the valley in early darkness. Ana knew her time had come. She slipped away from her tent and made her way to the western side of Jericho. There in the shadows, she squatted in the shelter of a sycamore and gave birth to her child.

She pulled a black shawl from her shoulders and swaddled him in it—his first cries muffled by the howling wind. She shook with the horror of knowing what she must do next. Having a baby before marriage was a grievous sin and the consequences harsh. She must kill the baby and dispose of his body before returning to camp.

Near the West Gate, Ana could see the torchlights of the guardians patrolling the wall. Her heart pounded. She offered a silent prayer to her God and hurried across the dry moat and struck the heavy knocker against the iron gate.

Soon the gate clanged and squeaked open, and a giant stood before her. Ana fell back in awe. The giant was of immense height but slight of build, his face was gentle and his eyes kind. His head was much larger than those of her people—the back of his cranium elongated and considerably larger. His neck was slender and long, his facial features delicate and his skin alabaster.

The giant's kindly countenance allayed Ana's fears enough for her to speak. She uncovered the face of her newborn and pleaded, "Please take my baby into your care."

The giant was clearly moved at the sight of the innocent child and his desperate mother. Creases of concern rippled across his brow. *She is but a child herself,* he thought. His eyes filled with compassion, but he declined to take the child from her outstretched arms. He spoke softly to a female guardian at his side who went away quickly and returned with blankets and a basket of food.

But Ana wept all the loader and wailed, "Please, I beg of you, take my child into your protection."

It seemed to Ana that the woman guardian was arguing for her, but she could not understand what was being said.

In the language of the Nutafians, Uriel, the male guardian, replied, "We have accepted innocent children before from the warlike tribes. Being raised in Jericho will not purge them of their violent ways. Their nature is inborn, and they will corrupt the harmony of our peaceful society."

But the female guardian persisted, "A woman in our village gave birth to a stillborn today," she said. "She mourns deeply and wails for a baby to put to her breast."

Ana's baby cried and flailed his tiny arms about such that one fist worked its way loose from its wrap. When the female guardian stepped forward to look at the infant, Ana thrust the child into her arms. The guardian gently pulled the cover from the baby's face. As she did, the infant gripped her finger tightly sending a rush of tenderness surging through her being.

Thunder rumbled through the valley, and the first drops of rain touched the guardian's face when, in a spasmodic show of fury, a bolt of lightning lit the night sky. In the flash of light, she saw Ana running across the moat through the water that had begun to flood in from the mountainous regions to the west.

And so it was that the child came to be raised in Jericho. Willow, his adopted mother, named him Adam for his red skin. Coming to her at the precise moment she delivered a stillborn, she considered the child to be a precious gift of divine providence. "The angels from heaven have sent one of their own to heal my sorrow," she said, and the community accepted Adam as such.

Adam grew to be a vivacious child with black curly locks. He was smaller than the Nutafian children, and his head lacked the enlarged cranium, but the differences in physical appearance only made his mother love him all the more. As Adam grew, Willow noticed that the differences were more than physical. Adam enjoyed the blissful freedom of the Garden, but the games the children played were cooperative rather than competitive, and Adam soon became bored with them. However, when summer came and the sun warmed the Garden, Adam did love to swim in the spring-fed lake with the other children. He would swing out over the swimming hole on the rope suspended from a large oak tree and drop with a splash into the cold water with his playmates.

The other children noticed Adam's curious looks and ways, and although they were fascinated by his uniqueness, they did not know how to deal with his proclivity to chase the animals or throw stones at flocks of birds as they fed on the grain just to see them flutter up startled, so Adam found himself alone much of the time.

He was a happy little boy and full of life, but his mischievous behaviour troubled his mother. Adam showed resentment and jealously toward his younger siblings, and he could be sulky, defiant and contrary if he did not get his way. He lacked some aspects of sensory and conscious perception afforded the Nutafians by their larger brains, and sometimes he felt frustrated because he could not fully understand everything as they did.

For instance, there was one spring that welled up from the ground through the roots of a very old coniferous tree in the center of the city and flowed southward to where it disappeared under the wall. The tree was known as the *Tree of Life* and was considered sacred because of the special properties of its oil. Also, the water from the spring provided the drinking water for the nomadic herdsmen and hunter gathers that camped outside the city, and great care was taken not to pollute it in any way. This water could only be used for drinking or cooking—washing clothes, bathing or swimming in it was forbidden. Adam did not appreciate the importance of such measures. This troubled his mother greatly, and she admonished him repeatedly for swimming in it.

So when Adam's interest turned to the opposite sex, his mother hoped he had matured and his mischievous ways would be replaced with more responsible ways of the heart. She also hoped that having a mate would make him feel less isolated. In his teens, Adam's attention turned to one young lady in particular. Lilith was a vibrant classic beauty with long wavy raven hair and alabaster skin. She, in kind, found this strange rebellious boy attractive. Willow was pleased. If anyone could mold Adam, it would be Lilith.

In time, Adam and Lilith became mates and produced a beautiful baby girl who they named Eve—the name meaning 'descendent of the dark one'. Eve had the alabaster skin and dark tresses of her mother, but she lacked the large cranium, and she did not have her mother's boldness.

Where did she get her characteristics? Only the guardian at the gate the night Adam came to live in Jericho, knew. Uriel felt he had met her before. The special way she held her mouth and her facial features and expressions were those of the young woman who so desperately pleaded for sanctuary for her newborn baby sixteen years earlier.

Adam and Lilith's marriage was fraught with dissention from the beginning. They differed on so many fronts and quarreled constantly. Adam felt that he should dominate his wife—a concept unacceptable to Lilith and indeed foreign to everyone in the community. The Nutafians held women in high esteem. As the rift between Adam and Lilith deepened, Adam became more and more attached to his daughter. Eve never challenged his authority. Indeed, she was bone of his bone and flesh of his flesh, and the two became inseparable.

They were too close, Lilith thought—an opinion shared by Adam's mother, Lilith's parents and many others of the Garden. Alarmed by what she saw unfolding—the way Adam looked at Eve, and spoke to her and touched her—Lilith tried to reason with her husband, but he did not see anything wrong with his actions. He dismissed his wife's protestations out of hand and set about to turn his daughter against her mother. He told Eve that her mother resented the love he had for her. The fight then shifted to Eve and her mother with Eve saying hurtful things. Lilith tried to prevent Eve from being alone with her father, but Adam always found ways around this. Frantic and angry, Lilith became irritable and shouted at Adam, and her behavior convinced Eve that her mother was not a nice person. Lilith's efforts to prevent what she feared for Eve only served to alienate her further from her daughter.

Desperate, Lilith turned to Adam's mother for help. "I would help you," Willow said, "but Eve treats me the same way she treats you. Perhaps it will take the help of a man," She suggested. Uriel loves Adam as a son and has been watching his progression over the years. Adam looks up to him. Perhaps Uriel would be willing to intervene."

So one afternoon when Eve was planting grain in the fields with her mother, Uriel found Adam and drew him aside. As they walked through the palm groves and pistachio trees, Uriel counselled Adam. "You may partake of the fruit of any of the trees in the Garden, but there is one tree from which you must not partake. Your seed will produce forbidden fruit from her womb." Uriel spoke metaphorically of course, but as it was customary for the Nutafians to do so, Adam understood.

Adam knew what Uriel was saying; he had heard the same warning phrased in many different ways before, none so clearly as from his wife. He resented being criticized about his relationship with his daughter, and turned away, but Uriel laid his hand on Adam's shoulder and, looking into his eyes, said earnestly, "Adam, Eve is flesh of your flesh. It is a grievous sin for you to know her. It is an offense punishable by banishment. The penalty is harsh because incest will cause the demise of the entire City." Uriel's voice was grave. "Adam, you would not only be driven from the Garden to toil in the dessert, but Eve and the unborn child—your child—would also be driven out of Paradise too."

But Adam paid no heed to the desperate warnings. He partook of the forbidden tree, and they three—for Eve was three months along with child at the time—were driven from the Garden; they and their descendents banned from Paradise forever.

Lilith wailed and pleaded to be sent out of the Garden in Eve's place. She asked that she be allowed to care for the baby outside of the Garden so that Eve could remain in the paradise, but her request was denied, and Adam and Eve were led to the gate.

While they were in the Garden, Adam and Eve walked in bare feet, but when the gate opened, they saw that the earth outside was strewn with stones. They trembled with fear. They had only known the comfort and beauty of the Garden with all its fragrant trees laden with delicious fruit. How could they survive in such barren conditions? They fell on their faces and cried, but the guardians raised them up and led them to a place on the eastern boarder of Jericho under an overhanging rock—a place known as the Cave of Treasures.

Adam said, "Look at this cave. Is this to be our prison. It's gloomy, dark and cramped and it smells bad." He kicked the parched soil in disgust. "How can we live here when we're used to fertile soil and light and fragrance?" He didn't want to go into the cave, so he pummeled his breast until he dropped lifeless to the ground.

Eve thought he was dead and screamed," Adam, you can't leave me alone in this dungeon. I can't survive alone."

When Adam revived, he said to Eve," We must cover ourselves with dust and be remorseful and beg to be allowed back into Paradise."

He took Eve and went to the gate on the south wall of the City where they could smell the fragrance of the Garden being that the wind blows from the north. Near the gate, they found the water that springs from the ground under the roots of the Tree of Life in the center of the City. Here it flowed out of the Garden and split into four rivers.

When he was in the Garden, Adam did not see the Tree of Life's greatness. To him, it was just another tree with leaves that emitted a pleasant smell. He hadn't cared that the tree provided many health benefits and longevity or that it gave the skin a healthy glow or that it repelled insects. Most perilously of all, he had not appreciated the secret virtue of its oil. Now he trembled with the thought that he would never have eternal life.

Adam knelt down and drank from the water. It tasted pure and fresh, and he was filled with a great remorse for his recklessness. He tried to drown himself by throwing himself into the waters, but Eve implored him loudly once again not to leave her alone.

Then Adam told Eve, "Go to the gate and entreat them to let us in. They will see that you cannot survive in this harsh place being that you are with child."

Eve did as Adam asked, but the guardian at the gate said, "I have made you a promise that when five thousand and five hundred years is complete, I will bring you back into the Garden."

Faint from hunger, Adam searched the land for something to eat but found nothing that was not animal food. The riverbanks were thick with vegetation, but it was all thistles and thorns. There was no food to be found that they were used to eating, and they returned to the cave late into the evening.

Being that it was early spring, the nights were long and the rock overhang prevented any moonlight from getting in, so when they entered the cave, it was very dark. Adam could hear Eve, but he couldn't see her in the darkness, and he cried out. "Where are you Eve?"

Eve's voice trembled. "I'm here," she said, "standing alone in the darkness."

They were afraid of the darkness; it made them feel separated, and this deepened their sorrow. They had never experienced complete blackness before. In the Garden, oil lamps lighted the houses at night, and the outdoors was open to the night sky. Remembering the light of the city and the golden rods, Adam moaned. When he lived in Paradise, he did not appreciate their value. Now because he had not listened to the warnings, he had lost everything and he wanted to die. Overcome with grief and bitterness, he mourned through the long night until dawn.

By early light, Adam went up into the mountains and threw himself off a cliff, but he didn't die, he was only bruised and bleeding. So he went down to the River Jordan to drown himself. While he was in the water, Eve cried and pleaded, "Adam, do not leave me alone in this barren land. If you come out of the water, I will take the blame for your transgression."

So Adam came out of the Jordan and went again to the gate of the City where he beat his chest and begged the guardians to let them in. Adam's brothers Gabriel, Michael and Raphael had witnessed his attempts to kill himself, and came out of the Garden with incense, myrrh and golden rods to lift Adam's spirits—with goats and sheep also, and fig branches laden with fruit for Adam and Eve to eat. They did this mainly because of Eve—they were full of sorrow for her and knew she would need Adam now in order to survive.

Raphael said to Adam, "I've brought seeds for you to plant so you can have vegetables and fruit to eat."

But Adam was sullen and surly. "I don't know how to till the soil," he grumbled.

"We'll show you how," Gabriel said, and he, Michael and Raphael helped Adam establish a garden and an orchard.

Sorrow continued to weigh heavily on Adam, and he continued to repent and plead to be allowed back into the Garden. When that didn't work, he and Eve would lay in wait for a gate to open and try to sneak in, but guards were posted at each gate and they were vigilant.

By fall, it came time for Eve to deliver her baby, and she wanted her mother with her. Hoping if she were alone and about to give birth, she would be allowed back in the Garden to have her child, so she went to the west of Jericho to the area of the sycamore where Adam was born. She was in great distress and cried out loudly, "Mother, Mother! I need you," but no one heard her.

When Adam realized Eve was gone, he went in search of her. Finding her in great distress, he ran to the gate and pounded on it, and twelve luminaries came out of the Garden and attended Eve's delivery. Of those were Eve's two grandmothers and her mother. Willow wiped Eve's face with cool water and Lilith's mother stroked her back as Lilith prepared to deliver the baby. "Bear down," Lilith commanded Eve, and soon the first child was received into her hands. Lilith wrapped him in a sheepskin and laid him in Willow's arms as Eve gave birth to his twin sister.

From that day forward, Adam and Eve lived in the Cave of Treasures with their children and tilled the soil outside the garden. They had five children, two sets of twins and another son. Then Adam did not know his daughter in a carnal way again, although they lived together as a family.

Soon thereafter, Adam began to notice the women of the nomadic tribes who camped nearby and saw that they were beautiful. He had many more children by them. In all, Adam had thirty sons and thirty daughters.

Adam lived to be 930 years old, as measured in lunar years. Toward the end of his life, he became sick and in great pain and knew he was about to die, so he gathered his children about him.

Facing death, Adam once again became desperate to enter the Garden, for only in the Garden could his soul live on for eternity. Only in the Garden could he be anointed with the oil from the Tree of Life.

He sent Eve to the gate and instructed her to put dust on her head and throw herself on the ground and lament and ask for pity that he might be allowed to enter the Garden to die. But the guardian of the gate said to her, "Get up from the ground and weep and plead no more because in no way will Adam be allowed into the garden either before death or after."

Eve returned to the cave carrying with her sweet herbs of nard, crocus, calamus and cinnamon to anoint Adam, but she didn't have the oil from the Tree of Life. When she arrived at the cave and found that Adam's breath had gone out of him, she folded her hands over her head, bent over in agony and wept bitterly.

Having heard of Eve's visit to the Garden, Michael, Gabriel, Raphael arrived at the Cave of Treasures to find Eve wailing.

"We have come with linens, myrrh, aloes and cassia to prepare Adam's body," they said.

When the men finished binding the body, Eve said, "Lay him on the east side of the cave where the little bit of light comes in." They followed Eve's request and set up a table by Adam's head on which Eve placed a lamp so that he could have light, and they blew their trumpets.

Adam's soul left him at the ninth hour of the 15th day of March according to the epact of the sun. It was on the same date that Adam came out of the Garden.

A Wheel within a Wheel

I n a distant time,—before Gilgamesh and the Great Flood—the continent now known as Europe was home to a primordial people who tilled the soil in peaceful partnership. The Greek poet, Hesiod, referred to these people as the "Golden Race" and the land where they dwelt as the Garden of Eden. In the Dead Sea Scrolls, Enoch described them as angels, luminaries and giants. They were a sensuous, spontaneous people with a profound connection to the earth. Rich in mythology and folklore, their villages teemed with celebration, but this day—the day my story begins—trouble hung over paradise.

On this inauspicious day, Una had been pulled from the bustle of her little village of Kar-en-ach and summoned with immediate urgency to assemble at the Great Wheel. As she walked along the edge of the freshly harvested field toward the ocean cliff, the cacophonic cries of noisy gulls interrupted the tranquility of the ebbing tide that lapped against rocks below, while low on the horizon, the moon appeared in the sky before dusk. Una knew well the ways of the moon and stopped to gaze on his magnificent face. She marveled at the contours on its surface, how incredibly close this heavenly body was to earth and its power over her earth's oceans. The moon orbited the earth twice for every sunrise, and this moon was in its first quarter. Not a full moon, but still she could feel its tug on the waters within her—the brine that spilled from her eyes and moistened her white cheeks, the milk that was soon to flow in her breasts, the waters of her womb and the blood that surged through her veins like a rushing spring torrent from a mountain stream.

Una had been preparing for the evening's festivities and so was dressed in her finery. A golden snake coiled around her upper arm—a gift crafted by her mother on the occasion of her first lunar blood. Around her slender neck hung a necklace of spirals and chevrons, and a linen dress, ornately woven by her mother's sister and gifted to her on the same occasion, fell loosely over her swollen belly. A wreath of fresh white flowers adorned her titian hair. Una presented an imposing figure, tall, vibrant and fresh, with alabaster skin and pale blue eyes so pure and strange. Una did not see herself as beautiful because she did not see in her reflection what others saw— the spontaneous smile, the hint of mystery about her and the charming way she held her mouth when engaged in conversation. She was comfortable in this modern world of agriculture so filled with mysticism and knowledge. For her, everything in the universe was intriguing, the sounds of nature, the celestial bodies in the heavens and all things of the earth whether living or cold.

Trying to prolong the period of not knowing, Una turned back towards her village that lie beyond the fruit groves and harvested fields. Cradled in the sprawling valley below, a continuous spiral of houses radiated from the center of town. Smoke curled heavenward from the outdoor hearths and bread ovens, and music rose from the temple as the women of the village prepared a feast for their guests. The equinox fell on this day; it was a time of great jubilation. Almost all the crops were in, and villagers from every part of the land arrived in Kar-en-ach with oxen-driven carts laden with the gifts of their bounty—pottery, baskets, textiles, seeds, medicinal herbs, honey and all manner of animals and fruits of the sea. They came to celebrate, visit kin and friends and to share knowledge. The villagers took great pride in gifting their best to neighbours and received the same in return. The land was fertile; there was always enough of everything for all, and temple vaults bulged with the surpluses. Many found mates during these celebrations, and the men would leave their villages and reside in the home of their mates. This provided security and support for women in childbirth and childrearing as their mothers, aunts and sisters always surrounded them—it also meant that Kar-en-ach would lose some of its sons to other villages, but they were also to gain new ones.

From her distant vantage point, Una recognized her father's brother, Barakel, and his mate, Ash-rah as they arrived with their two little girls. Una wanted to run to them and embrace them, but she would not.

Coming from the far northern reaches of the land, her father's kin were often the first to arrive, anxious to taste of the sweet fruit of the groves and vineyards in the south. This year, they would stay for a full lunar cycle to partake in the lament for her mother. Ash-rah would stay on longer to aid in the birth of Una's child. Una knew they had received word of her mother's death, but probably not of her father's shame or of his banishment.

She remembered her father taking her to visit the caves of his ancestors in the direction of winter's low rising sun. How beautiful were the walls and ceilings with paintings; the rock face breathed life into the antelope and bison so artfully depicted there. She felt the high regard her father held for the

grotto as he reverently explained the meaning of the paintings to her. It was as though he had entered a sacred place;
he was not at that time of body, but of spirit. That image of
him remained carved in Una's mind as vividly and as permanently as the bulls on the cave wall. This made it all the
more difficult to understand his actions. She could not look
at her father after learning of his transgression and didn't see
the remorse in his face or the pleading for forgiveness in his
eyes as he left the village. His cart filled with supplies, he was
driven out of the land forever, banished to the far away land
of the war-like tribes with their male gods.

For the first time in her fifteen years, Una knew fear. It
came out of the primal shadows and struck with the force
of a lightening bolt. Yes, she was sad at the death of her
mother, shocked and bewildered by the deeds of her father,
but fear was a new passion in her. She had always been happy,
had always felt safe. Surrounded by an abundance of love,
folktales, songs and dance, she knew the liturgy of nature,
and she was secure; she had a song with her. Now sensing a
pending devastation about to befall her village, to threaten
the very existence of this vast land that she loved so much,
she felt exposed to the savage uncertainties of the future. It
could mean only one thing for her to be summoned with such
urgency to the Great Wheel. Why now? Why in the midst of
all else? She questioned her strength and her power to face it,
and her body trembled.

Across the moor, at the center of the vast rows of menhirs
and dolmens, sunlight glistened off the white quartz exterior
of the cairn where the silk-draped body of her mother lay in
preparation for passage. Beside the path, butterflies flitted in
and out of the shrubbery. In the field below, a goat meandered through a grove; his nose turned upward as he looked

longingly at the fruit hanging just beyond his reach. Then Una noticed something that changed her mood for the better and brought it into alignment with this idyllic setting. In the shade of a fruit tree, a young auroch calf lay as his mother grazed nearby. Una reasoned the young calf was only a few months old, probably born late in spring, maybe even early summer, as his coat color had not completely changed to deep brown yet, but the defining white eel stripe was beginning to show along his spine. The cow's reddish brown figure moved languorously as her beige muzzle and pale mouth mowed the domesticated grass. The ancient beast exhibited a confidence that announced this pasture belonged to her and to her calf. There was no doubt that she felt safe here as she availed herself of the plentitude of modern-day grains. It was exciting and a very good omen to see this primitive animal with her long horns and black curly forelocks, this wild forbearer of their modern-day domesticated cattle and oxen, this vestige from the past. Una had only seen these magnificent beasts depicted on the walls of her father's cave. And here they were, inserting themselves into humankind's manipulated world, as if to say we were becoming too boastful, too prideful of our accomplishments, too arrogant in our assumption that we could take command of their world.

Something stirred in the stubble near Una's feet, and she peered into the shadows. A head turned in her direction, and two lidless eyes stared up at her. The writhing serpent goddess, protector of the village, rubbed her body against a brittle shaft of grain in an effort to free herself from the skin she had outgrown.

A sense of peace descended like a warm spring rain, and Una realized that just as the earth becomes pregnant in spring and gives birth in season, she too held the sacred gift of regeneration, her power in water and stone, in tomb and cave. Filled with renewed courage, she continued along the path towards the peak. She reached the summit to find all the celestial sages gathered around the Great Wheel. Una had spent many days at this site—being taught the knowledge of the cosmos by her mother from as early as she could remember, and a profound sadness overcame her. This place held for her mother what the caves held for her father. It was a sacred place, a place connected to all the heavenly bodies in the sky.

The observatory stood on a lofty mountain of flint hard rock overlooked the ocean with a clear view of both the eastern and western horizons. It resembled a wheel within a wheel. The center post on the eastern perimeter of the wheel aligned with sunrise at equinox and a post on the western perimeter where the sun set that same day. This set down the east-west equatorial axis. An additional six posts on the eastern perimeter—three to the south of the equatorial axis and three to the north—framed six portals in which the sun rose. The sun rose and set either thirty or thirty-one times in each portal. This pattern was reflected on the western perimeter by six portals in which the sun set. The moon also rose and set in these portals, as did the stars, all following in corresponding order. Each portal was divided into smaller sections called gates, but not all the portals had the same number of gates. The portals nearest to the east-west line had twelve gates and were referred to as "The Great Portals." These were the largest of the portals because the sun moves faster along the horizon either side of the equinox. The next portals outwards had eight gates, and the extreme outer portals had only four. The portals were numbered from one to six from south to north. This configuration made up the inner wheel—the diameter of the inner wheel being one hundred megalithic yards.

An outer wheel encircled the inner at a further distance of fifty megalithic yards. Large posts in the outer wheel aligned with the gates in the inner wheel, and smaller posts separated each gate into sections called windows. There were 366 windows in the outer wheel—the exact number of sunrises in one year. The sun rose in the heavens through each eastern window in succession and set in its corresponding window in the west on the same day. The Great Wheel could track any bright object in the sky by its angle of inclination with the horizon.

This day, all the village astronomers gathered at the fourth portal. They listened intently as the Guardian, Anahita, talked excitedly about her observations. A few wisps of hair whipped her rosy cheeks; the wind had pulled them loose from the braids that adorned the crown of her long curly locks. Anahita had the same pure blue eyes as Una, but hers were a striking contrast to her dark complexion. Una always admired Anahita's beauty, no less so today even though her smile was absent and her words solemn. "I have witnessed a blazing fire, which runs without resting and does not flag in its course, holding to it equally by day and by night," Anahita announced.

Una understood that all the heavenly bodies move in a precise path in accordance with their journey through the cosmos moving from one portal to another in succession. Only a "Wandering Star" would disobey movement along each succeeding portal—and it was coming right at earth.

It was clear to everyone that the Great Wheel was finally fulfilling the main purpose for which it had been built. For millennia, the observatory had provided Una's people with a calendar that informed them when to put seeds into the earth, to breed their livestock and to host fertility rites. But today, they observed what they feared most—a great fireball of destruction.

"We must give heed to know with regards to when and where this fireball will wreak its destruction on the earth," one observer said, and some immediately took up long cords and hurried off to the north to take further measurements.

Another observer raised the question of the visitors. "Consider those who have come from afar to our village," she said. "This night must be joyous, it being the time of heavenly wonder." So it was decided that the villagers would not be informed of the looming cataclysm until the next day.

The seriousness of the moment was shattered as Una's name rang out across the summit, and two breathless little girls flung themselves into her arms. "We have come with gifts to offer you," they chimed excitedly. And, pointing to Una's abdomen, "Can we listen to the baby?" they giggled. One pressed her head against Una's belly, and the other crowded into her side. Their warmth and excitement drove the dark clouds from Una's mind. The gathering was about to form their circle of love as they always did to end an assembly. Inside the Great Wheel, they all joined hands and raised their voices in harmony as they sang the words of love, unity and peace. Una felt the warmth of the two small hands in hers and saw the joy that seeped back into the faces of her colleagues as they watched the excitement on the fresh little faces.

The two little girls skipped and chattered relentlessly as they pulled their cousin down the path to the village, and their merriment restored balance to Una's life. The birds chirped louder, and the ocean laughed.

Ash-rah watched expectantly as the trio neared, and she ran to greet them. Una's mate, Raguel, was helping Barakel lift barrels of live shellfish from his cart. Barakel had set his barrel down to take another bite of fruit when he saw them arrive. After joyful embraces, enquiries as to her health and pregnancy and condolences on the loss of her mother, Ash-rah and Barakel pulled Una excitedly toward their cart, to the gifts they could scarcely wait to bestow on her. Raguel leaned against the wagon with his easy smile and watched as the gifts were presented. He had seen them already and wanted to see the expression on his mate's face when she saw them. There was a woven basket for the child, lined with goose-down-filled hand painted silk and beautiful pottery shaped like the curvature of a pregnant belly and adorned with white swans whose graceful long necks tucked their heads into their chest, all against a background of colorful wavy lines and glyphs. There was also a large wooden bowl carved from sacred oak and a beautiful figurine of the Creatrix with her swollen belly and breast above a prominent vulva.

There were tears of joy and tight embraces, as no words could express the gratitude Una felt for their generosity and the depth of love that the gifts embodied. She would treasure these gifts with the same passion she had for the figurine they gifted at her mating celebration. That figurine was of a beautiful young woman in a sitting position with her arms around her knees displaying the full sensuality of her vulva. It spoke of the passion and desire she had felt for her mate. Within the month Una became with child.

As Raguel carried the treasures to their dwelling, Ash-rah reached beneath a blanket in the cart. "The sisters of Barakel will not take such a journey this equinox," she explained. "Ker-id-win is nearing delivery, and Babatha will stay with her for the birth. They send good wishes and gifts. From Babatha, a bunting bag for the child." Ash-rah passed the garment to Una, who sunk her face into the soft rabbit fur.

"From Ker-id-wen, a pair of winter shoes for you and Raguel," Ash-rah glowed as she pulled the gifts from her cart. The shoes were made from goat hides, adorned with snakeskin and lined with rabbit fur.

"And I have gifts for all," Una wiped tears from her eyes. She felt overwhelmed. "But it seems no matter what I gift, I get back ten thousand fold."

With the wonderful smells of fresh bread and the roasted goat being taken from the fire pit, Barakel was eager to get to the temple to partake of the feast. "Edible love," he smiled. "I could smell it as we approached the village. Nothing says welcome like the smell of sumptuous food after a fortnight's journey."

This night, Una would push her dismal thoughts aside and enjoy the vibrant celebration—except for one thing. Before the meal Una would have to explain the absence of her father—of his expulsion from the land forever. No need to provide further details. Only one sin was deserving of such drastic punishment. Even with murder, he would have been able to return after a time. But he had committed the ultimate sin. Barakel's and Ash-rah's reaction was one of shock and bewilderment just as Una's had been. Barakel in particular seemed overly subdued during the feast, keeping mostly to himself and only taking part in the revelry when it was foisted upon him. Una's father and Barakel had another brother, Shalem, who was celebrating the holiday with kin in another village. Barakel must accept the difficult task of informing Shalem when he arrived in Kar-en-ach later.

The feast was over before sunset, and the orator began to recount the ancient legend of the massive fireball from the heavens. Usually Una loved to hear the storyteller relate the tale, but tonight it only heightened her anxiety.

In a far-off memory, a time before we tilled the earth, a wandering star lit up our sky with the brightness and heat of ten suns. It splashed down into the ocean and unleashed its catastrophic furor. Such were the extremes of temperature and pressure on the earth that any surviving man or beast was rendered deaf and speechless. Great walls of brackish water flooded the lands, energy fields convulsed, earth's belly ruptured, and a frenzied earth spewed up molten lava. The resulting firestorms claimed all variety of living things. The earth lay in stunned silence, her energy alignment shattered. Fowl, butterflies, all creatures of the air and of the deep became confused, and they could not find their course of journey either in flight or by sea.

But out of the chaos came awakening. The few who survived came out of their caves, ceased the shedding of blood and lawlessness and worked together to right the earth from the angry celestial forces. They settled into villages on the moor, tilled and planted the earth, cultivated silk worms, raised honeybees, domesticated animals and aligned the stones. Male and female— all with their eyes on the sky—dedicated their lives to restoring balance to the earth.

We are their children. We must stay steadfast and ever watchful.

As the legend ended, the festivities of the equinox began, and the night filled with enchantment. A full moon cast its magic over the moor and sprinkled cosmic dust over the endless rows of menhirs and obelisks that held the cosmos and earth energies together. The megaliths fluoresced blue in the moonlight. Heavenly constellations winked dimly like a myriad of eyes watching the festivities below, but high in the night sky, outshining the celestial sphere, the ringed planet fixed his steely gaze on the unwary merrymakers. Earth energy currents running though the sacred site caused the air to radiate a feeling of anticipation. Bonfires burned, and maidens danced with complete abandon between the stones that loomed large under the night sky. Garlands of flowers adorned their hair, and some wore only jewelry over their chests exposing their breasts. They danced the ritual dance that celebrated the sanctity of menarche. Some would choose a mate tonight just as Una had done at the spring equinox.

When the festivities drew to a close, Una sat with her mate watching the dying embers of the fire. Raguel put his hand under her chin and raised her face to his. "What wrestles with your heart tonight, Beloved?" he enquired.

Looking into Raguel's large gentle eyes, Una realized that she could accept whatever was to transpire as long as he was by her side. "Naught that cannot wait for sunrise," she said. She smiled into his eyes and laid her head against his breast. The secret could wait.

The next morning, a meeting of the council of astrological affairs was called. Anahita, her mate, Uriel, and their son, Nephilim, along with six women met to decide what action must be taken. All the village people were invited to attend. Those with specific knowledge of earth's energy lines and those with agricultural expertise would be needed. The consensus was that the time of impact could be predicted but not where the fireball would strike.

From the legend, they understood the effects that this event would have. Once the tidal waves receded, there would be a prolonged cold dark winter during which time nobody would see the passage of the seasons. After the dust settled, which could take ten years, survivors would need to recreate a calendar if they were to have a good chance of reestablishing agriculture. Because they could not determine where the impact would take place—indeed it could wipe their own culture out completely—the people decided to spread their knowledge as widely as possible. Scouts were sent out to recruit patriarchs from friendly tribes to the south. One of those recruited was Enoch from the district of Qumran. Since the tribal people they sought to educate were patriarchal and held no respect for women, the council decided only men from the village would interact with the outsiders.

Over the following weeks, many villagers made ready to seek the safety of higher ground further inland. Bonfires burned late into the night, and caravans departed every day. Cows pulled the carts, and goats and sheep walked alongside.

Una's brother, Azazel, hung back as long as he could. He was concerned for Una and wanted to be with her to grieve the loss of their mother. Azazel's mate and their sons had gone on ahead with her family. On the last morning before his departure, the small group of mourners that were left in the village joined arms and danced the Dance of Lament for Una's mother; Una wept for her father as well. Sparks from the bonfires crackled through the early morning mist, as the mourners circled the great oak and wound their way through the stone alignments singing the Song of Lament and feeling the fullness of their loss.

The mourners were left with a feeling of emptiness after the lament. It seemed so final. Reluctant to leave, Azazel walked across the moor with Una to visit the dolmen where their mother's body would be laid to rest after passage. He said his goodbyes to his little brother whose resting place this had been for the last four years. Their brother had scarcely seen his fifth winter solstice when he succumbed to an illness that ravaged the village that season. Alone on the moor together, the siblings discussed for the first time the consequence of their brother's death. Something changed in their father. He became hard and distant. The rest of the family, in their own grief, hadn't noticed it at first. Their mother, heartbroken, visited the dolmen everyday, and it seemed that their parent's love for each other died with the death their son. Then when their mother died so suddenly, their father became exceptionally strange; there was something savage in his eyes.

That evening, fog hung pungent in the air. Azazel slung two sacks of seed grain into the back of his cart beside beehives and supplies. He took up the driver's seat, and Una watched with heavy heart as the cart disappeared into the murky night. The journey would not be an easy one. Winter was fast approaching.

The men who had been charged with teaching outsiders the secrets of their advanced culture stayed behind. Una also remained with her husband, her mother's sisters and Ash-rah who would attend the birth.

By the eve of solstice, the village was mostly empty. The outsiders had returned to their homelands, and snow blanketed the landscape. Una left the warmth of her hearth and crossed the moor to the dolmen; the imprints of her winter shoes left their imprint in the frost. Winter birds flew overhead and landed on a shrub to eat the fermented red berries. The standing stones gave off a low vibration of energy, and Una felt their connection to the forces of the earth. Her pains were becoming increasingly frequent now, and she felt warm water spill from her womb.

Chants of earth tones swelled from the mound of earth to the south and echoed through the passageways as the attendants adorned the silk-draped corpse of Una's mother with red ochre and placed cowry shells around her. Una made her way to the vaulted central chamber and lay down on the birthing bed. Behind the ornate curbstone above the main door, light from the Morning Star streaked into the chamber bathing everything in a pale silvery glow. The attendants chanted the ancient Earth Song asking the Earth Goddess to carry the soul of Una's mother to the infant. The sound resonated within the massive stones and echoed the murmurings of the earth itself. A harmony was struck between the celestial, the earth, the stones and the people like a super choir—each voice distinct but all in perfect synchrony. Just as the light from the solstice sun cast its first rays on the wall of the central chamber, the gentle cry of a newborn baby transcended the heavenly chorus.

That same day, a wandering star impacted earth on the shores of a distant continent to the southeast in the district of Qumran. The Great Wheel was spared, and Una's people lived on in peace.

The Day the Sun Stood Still

Off the northwest coast of Brittany, an isthmus juts some 14 kilometers into the Atlantic Ocean. White sandy beaches flank the narrow strip of land barely wide enough for a highway and a railway line. Forty kilometers to the north lies the small island of Téviec. The obscure island would be of little interest if it were not for the archeological grave sites unearthed there and the mystery surrounding remains buried in the middens of oyster and clam shells. Three of the skeletons tell a story of violence and murder that occurred in this area 6500 years ago. One has an arrowhead embedded in his spine, but the most famous of these findings are the "Ladies of Téviec." Two women in their early thirties were buried together in one grave, their remains lovingly protected by antler bones and adorned with seashell jewelry. One skull shows five severe blows to the head and an arrow between her eyes. The other died of a brutal beating. The degree of violence in a place that was thought to be a quiet, goddess worshiping settlement at the time of the murders has archeologists baffled.

The women are believed to be from the nearby village of Carnac, renowned for its prehistoric stone alignments, dolmens and tumuli. Carnac was a vibrant, agricultural community at the time rich in artwork, passage chambers and stone circles that tell the story of a tranquil way of life.

Replicas of the Ladies of Téviec are laid out on a mortuary slab in the Muséum de Toulouse, and the curator is asking for help from the public to solve this ages old murder mystery.

Some suggestions include violent raids to steal food during a time of famine, meteorological phenomena and sacrificial offerings. None of these explanations fit prehistorical facts or Marija Gimbutas's description of the civilization that occupied Old Europe.

It is widely accepted that this civilization was wiped out by a very violent male dominated tribe from the Russian Steppes who Gimbutas dubbed the Kurgans. But that did not happen until two thousand years after the murders at Téviec.

I would like to offer a hypothetical account that would fit the archeological findings of Gimbutas and her Kurgan theory.

Old Europeans are renowned for their sophisticated knowledge of astronomy as evidenced by the plethora of celestially aligned stone monuments all over the British Isles and Brittany. Indeed, the cluster of archeological sites at Brú na Boinne in Ireland have been called a Stone Age university of observational astronomy. The oldest of the main passage tombs there, Dowth, its name meaning darkness, is famous for its study of solar eclipses. Dowth itself holds an unsettling history of its own, so it is fitting that this place of infamy should figure into my story. I have woven David Baron's description of a total solar eclipse into my narrative. In a TED talk, Baron describes this rare cosmic event as "the most awe-inspiring spectacle in all of nature."

This is my proposal of what happened that fateful day.

It all took place on summer solstice of the year 4625 BCE, this being the day the sun stands still on the horizon before reversing direction and moving back to its position at winter solstice. The crops were in the ground, and the people were enjoying the lazy dog days of summer. Celebrations were in full swing in the village.

This was not an ordinary summer solstice. This year was special. For on this day the moon was in its new phase and also on the line of the ecliptic. Both meet the conditions for a total solar eclipse to cut a 100 kilometer wide swath across the Carnac region. Many astronomers from the complex of observatories to the north had descended on the community with their pinhole viewing boxes to witness this incredible event. They arrived a few days earlier to instruct the villagers how to safely view the eclipse. Looking directly at the sun can cause blindness, but during the three to seven minutes of totality it is safe to view the sun with the naked eye. A drumroll would let everyone know when the moon had fully eclipsed the sun and another would announce that it was time to view indirectly again.

One woman renowned for her studies of solar eclipses at Dowth was among the honored guests. I will call her Mari. She and her childhood friend from the village—who I will call Ana—frolicked this day in the surf under the late morning sun. Being that the sun beat relentlessly on the plages of Carnac, Mari and Ana decided to go for a quick swim in the Atlantic before the solar event. They dropped their linen frocks on the grass and ran across the white sand to where the water ebbed and flowed against the beach. Laughing, they splashed and kicked water on each other until they reached a depth where they could submerge. Mari dove under and surfaced, pulling her long red tresses back from her face just as the drumroll sounded over the community. The eclipse neared, and it was time to make their way to the bluff.

Above the drumroll rose a thundering sound, the vibrations of which could be felt. Most of the villagers were already on the summit, but one man was making his way towards the path that led to the bluff. Ana was pulling on her dress on the beach, but Mari had stopped near the shoreline. She stood frozen like a pillar of stone, her eyes wide as she tried to make out the aberration hurtling into sight from around the land mass to the north. Mari stared in disbelief. Horses had been wiped out in Europe at the height of the last ice age, so she had never seen one before. She thought the mounted men were some sort of strange man-beasts.

Mari did not notice the villager fall to the ground with an arrow in his back as he ran towards the path. Hers was a peaceful people. Never in all the 35 years of her life had she reason to suspect danger or fear brutality from those of her own species, so she stood motionless trying to make sense of what she saw.

Coming rapidly toward her were the strangest of all creatures she had ever seen. They had four sturdy large legs and two smaller ones, and the man-beasts had two heads, one of a man and another of a beast. The strange mythical beings traveled at an unimaginable speed and soon drew up near to her. To her amazement the man part separated from the beast and ran towards her in a crazed frenzy, all the time yelling something in a language she could not understand. He was taller than any man she had ever seen and muscular, and his face was set in an angry glare. He swung his club and dealt Mari several violent blows to the head. The club made a sickening sound as it struck, and Mari sank to her knees in the sand.

"Mari, run." Ana ran towards her friend as another mounted man clubbed her, and she fell face down. The frothy tide washed her blood from the sand.

Mari continued to look into the man's face. He too stopped dead in his tracks locked in the naked woman's gaze. Her red hair was matted with the blood that streaked her white cheeks, but her strange blue eyes conveyed an absence of fear. He saw only puzzlement.

As the eclipse drew near, weird things began to happen. A cool wind blew in from the ocean, and the world looked very strange. Shadows were bizarrely sharp, and it was starting to get so dark that the assailant thought his eyesight was failing. Just then, an arrow struck the woman who knelt in the sand before him. It entered her forehead right between her eyes, and caused the Kurgan's large body to lurch. Mari fell backwards and rolled onto her side in the sand, her eyes wide open. Those fearless blue eyes were the last thing the Kurgan saw. Suddenly complete darkness fell.

The Kurgan looked up into the blackened sky and roared for his Sun God to return. To his wonderment he found himself in a world he had never seen before—a world in which an entire day existed all at once. A sunset rimmed the entire horizon, and above the reds and oranges the sky was the deep purple grey of twilight, and above the dusk bright stars and planets shone in a night sky. A shimmering wreath hung majestically in the sky above him. The Moon Goddess had blocked out the light of the Sun God, and She wore a magnificent crown declaring Her dominance over the masculine. The regal headdress was not of gold and precious stones, but was finely textured and woven from strands of silk. Three bright planets orbited Her.

A sense of perfect peace fell over the Kurgan. For a brief moment he understood the woman he had just slain, and it would change who he was forever. He stood frozen in time staring at the sky until suddenly the sun burst out from behind the moon. His eyes remained steadfastly fixed on the event taking place in the sky. His eyes burned and tears wet his cheeks. He and his entire band of marauding savages stood awestruck staring at the sun as it emerged from behind the moon. When daylight returned to the earth, they found their mounts and fled.

They returned to their homeland blind, crazed and raving about how the moon ate the sun and caused a darkness to fall over the earth. They ranted of a land to the west and the supernatural powers of the people who lived there, of a witchcraft so powerful that it could alter the very universe and strike invaders blind.

Their story spread fear throughout their land and became legend that would be passed down for generations to come.

And so it was that the peaceful people of Old Europe were not set upon for another two thousand years.

Night Duty Room at the Hospital

It happened during my days as a blood bank tech at the hospital in the sixties and seventies. In those days, we were rather short staffed and so after working a full day we would take turns being on call from five in the afternoon until eight o'clock the next morning. Normally, I would go home and come back if called, but this day there was a blinding snowstorm on the east coast. That morning, armed with studded winter tires and two bags of sand I had loaded into the trunk of my '78 Cordova, I was the only blood bank tech to make it into work. I wasn't supposed to be on call that night but since the roads were so bad and I was already at the hospital, I offered to sleep in the night duty room.

Now you have to understand that for some reason when hospitals are designed absolutely no thought is given to the lab techs that must work there. We are always stuck in the basement, with no windows or ventilation and always across from the morgue. This was the case in this new hospital. Not only were we in the basement with the morgue but at the rear of the hospital. It meant that if I wanted to run some errands on my thirty minute lunch break I would go out to the back parking lot through the door at the rear of the hospital. This was the same door through which copses on gurneys were transported to and from the morgue. Thirty minutes was just enough time to run some errands on the fly as the hospital was located near the downtown core where the main shopping mall, my bank and a liquor store were located. But it meant that, rushing back into work I often had to squeeze through the poor past a corpse on a trolley. There was no time for respect for the dead.

To digress a moment — when I left the medical tech field at the hospital and went into medical research at the university, I thought I had left the basement labs behind. But in the health sciences research center next to a large teaching hospital in western Canada, my lab was once agin in the basement with no windows and right across from the morgue. Bodies coming and going were a routine part of the day. Sometimes when business was particularly busy at the morgue, stretchers carrying the bodies were lined up along the hall opposite our lab. The fact that our "lunch room" consisted of a long wooden table on the other side of the hallway between the freezers and refrigerators that had been moved out into the hallway to make space for the ever expanding array of new sophisticated equipment, compounded their pleasantry. I preferred to eat my lunch facing the stark cement block wall rather than facing the cadavers.

Anyway, the story I was going to tell you took place that stormy winter night in the east coast hospital. I was in a deep sleep when the phone rang. The night duty room consisted of a narrow room with two bunk beds and a small desk that the phone sat on. I always slept on the bottom bunk. The bunk was just long enough and wide enough to house my body. It was very much the dimensions of a casket but without the comfortable satin cushions the cadaver get to lie on. The fact that the top bunk closed in the space above me completed the feeling of being in a coffin. When the phone rang I jumped up, forgetting where I was and banged my head on the rail of the top bunk. I answered the phone with a hello that sounded more like a question than a greeting. The chipper voice on the other end said, "This is Third West calling and we have a stat Group and Cross for you."

The cheerfulness in the nurse's voice always irritated the hell out of me. I took it personally. I was sure it was directly attributable to the glee she got out of calling me in the middle of the night and disturbing my blissful sleep. And why couldn't nurses speak proper blood bank anyway? No one in the lab calls it a Group and Cross. It's a bloody crossmatch for Christ's sake — no pun intended.

"Okay," I mumbled. Feeling the lump on my forehead grow as I returned the receiver to the cradle without the courtesy of a thank you or a goodbye. I pushed my bare feet into my slippers and stood up in the dark room. I would just go down to the lab and pull a lab coat on over my pajamas. My hair wasn't combed and I hadn't brushed my teeth, but I was unlikely meet anyone anyway. Perhaps, I thought, this way I won't completely wake up in the 45 minutes it takes to do a crossmatch. Then maybe I could get back to sleep afterward.

I stepped into the dark hallway. The EXIT sign over the door that led out to the back parking lot provided dim illumination. I could have sworn that the door to the morgue just swung shut. I stood staring at it, my foggy brain trying to focus. There had been cases of people hiding out in the deep recesses of the hospital. Perhaps someone from the Psych ward or someone who had escaped police custody in Emerg was hiding here, or maybe an orderly had brought down a recently deceased cadaver. I stood staring at the door waiting for it to open again. Could it have been my imagination? I turned and headed down the hall toward the lab. I would call security from the lab. My pace picked up and shivers ran down my spine as I realized how vulnerable I was in this remote part of the hospital. The closest sign of life would be in the emergency ward located at the front of the hospital and one floor up. With the storm, it would be unlikely to find any other lab tech in tonight. I regretted telling the girl from chemistry that I would take her calls tonight so she could leave early yesterday afternoon.

I stopped to pick up the blood sample at the dumbwaiter but it was empty. The carriage of the dumb waiter was on the lab floor so the ward hadn't even called for it yet. I rounded the corner into the blood bank. The light in the blood fridge cast an aura of "off-hours" in the otherwise dark room. I reached for the light switch and was startled by the figure of a person standing motionless in the dark. I turned to face her and realized that it was just the skeleton that we had hung on an IV stand and dressed in a lab coat, latex gloves, face mask and safety glasses. It was supposed to be down in the lecture room. What was it doing in the blood bank of all places? It wasn't here when I left this afternoon.

The blood sample was lying on the lab bench. Very strange. The orderly must have walked it all the way over here. Must be a slow night on Third West. I picked up the requisition and read: *42 year old male. Anemia. Request 2 units of blood.*

Some stat, I thought, feeling a bit annoyed. A ruptured aorta, placenta previa, incomplete abortion, ectopic pregnancy, gun shot wound, car accident — those were stats — even a bloody nose. But anemia? And only two units? Some intern must have been snowed in here tonight and so bored he decided to order blood.

I centrifuged the specimen, set up the crossmatch and sat down to write up the paper work while the tests incubated. I must have been spooked because I jumped when the phone rang. It was Emerg.

"Could you come over and draw a blood sample? The intern can't seem to get it."

"Sure, be right over," I said wondering how they would know to phone the lab and not the night duty room. Maybe they tried the night duty room and when they got no answer, tried the lab. I figured that the patient in Emerge might be more of a stat than Mr. Anemia from Third West, so I started to head over to the Emergency department. Then I remembered I was in my pajamas and changed direction. I hurried down the hall to the night duty room and thought I say a light under the door to the morgue. What's going on in the morgue? I didn't have time to wonder about it at the time. I pulled some clothes on, ran a comb through my hair and stepped back out into the hallway. There was no light on under the morgue door. Once again I wondered if I had just imagined it.

By this now I was wide awake and remembered that I had forgotten to call security. I would feel better if security was down here checking things out, and I thought I had best call them and let someone know that I was concerned about strange going's on before walking through the dark deserted maze of hospital hallways and stairwells to the emergency department. I stopped at the blood bank and dialed the number for security but the phone rang and rang and there was no answer. Of course this was in the days before answering machines and voice mail. I had hoped the phone would bounce back to the hospital switchboard so I could at least leave a message with her, but that didn't happen. I started to ring emergency but thought I would sound like a silly spooked little girl afraid of the dark. I hung up, picked up my blood collection tray and headed down the dark hallway past the lab manager's office, past the hallway that lead into the X-ray department, past the Dietician's office, the kitchen, past a hallway leading to day surgery and pushed open the door to the stairwell that would take me up to the emergency department. Hearing the door band shut behind me, I realized that I might not be able to get out again. The door could be locked after hours for security reasons. Usually I walked down the long corridor through the boiler room area to the elevator at the front of the hospital, but tonight I was so anxious to get out of the basement I took the stairs. It was with a great sense of relief that the door opened into the well lit main floor of the hospital and I could hear the hum of activity coming from the end of the hallway in the waiting room.

It was unusually busy for this time of night. What time of night was it? I hadn't even thought to look. I peered into the waiting room and looked for a clock. Four am. It would soon be morning. The thought of daybreak gave me a sense of relief. As I turned back to the corridor, I realized that there were two policemen in the sitting room standing on either side of a man who appeared to be inebriated — well actually it was one policeman and a policewoman.

I headed down to the emergency desk. There was no one at the nursing station. I turned and looked out the emergency room doors while I waited. The storm had not abated, and I could see the yellow flashing light of a snowplow through the blowing snow. Of course they must be trying to keep access to the hospital open. I notice that the lights on the Christmas tree and the nativity scene outside the emergency department doors were out. We must be on auxiliary power. My thought were interrupted by a female voice behind me.

"Oh good, I hope you are the girl from the lab," a frenzied nurse said as she hurried towards me. "Come this way." She ushered me into the emergency ward and pulled back a curtain behind which stood a stretcher with the body of a young woman on it. "The intern ordered blood and he couldn't seem to get a blood sample. We need four units of blood and stat. She's lost a lot of blood." Then as quickly as the nurse materialized, she disappeared.

I moved around to the right side of the stretcher and laid out my supplies. The woman must be unconscious, I thought, because she lay motionless on the stretcher with her eyes wide open but seemingly not seeing anything. Her body was limp. I lifted her arm to wrap the tourniquet around it and was startled to realize that she felt cold to the touch. I wondered if she was even alive. Surely they would have checked for pupil dilation. I inserted the needle into the vein and pulled back on the plunger. No blood entered the syringe. I felt faint. I was definitely in the vein, but of course if the patient were dead, I wouldn't be able to draw any blood. There would be no blood pressure. I returned to the nursing station and said to the nurse, "I think the patient may be deceased and has been for some time. Her body is cold and I can't get any blood even though I'm in the vein. Could you check her?"

The nurse looked flustered but took her flashlight and hurried into the room.

"Pretty busy tonight?" I asked.

"Well, very short staffed because of the storm. There were just two of us on the ward tonight but now the head nurse is nowhere to be found. Something very mysterious is going on around her tonight," she said. "A car accident come in about an hour ago. There were only two patients in the ambulance. One was pronounce D.O.A. and the orderly took her down to the morgue. I was busy with the other patient but I heard the head nurse having an altercation with the intern. That's the last time I saw her. Now this new patient has turned up on the ward and I don't know where she came from or who brought her in. I didn't even know she was here until about ten minutes ago when the intern ordered blood for her."

The nurse shone the light in the patient's eyes. "I'm not getting any dilation of her pupils," she said. "I think you're right. I better get the doctor."

She left and came back a few minutes later with the intern. He was angry and ordered me to try again. Reluctantly I inserted the needle into the dead woman's arm again. "I'm definitely into the vein," I said, "but not getting any blood."

"Try the back of her hand," he barked. He held the skin taut over the veins in her hand.

I shook my head. "No, I'm sure she is dead, and I think she has been dead for some time because she is cold to the touch."

"Give me the syringe," he said angrily. "You hold the hand." I looked at the nurse who was desperately trying to convince him that the woman was dead. "Get the hand," he shouted at me.

I pulled the skin taut over the back of her hand and the intern inserted the needle into the vein. My legs were weak, and I though I might faint. The intern drew back on the plunger but no blood entered the barrel of the syringe. He became even more agitated.

"Get ready to do a cutdown on her vein," he shouted at the nurse.

My mind was whirling. Is he crazy? I snatched my tray and fled the room. In my frenzy to escape this macabre scene, I forgot to mention my concerns that someone was down in the lab area or to ask where the security guard was. I ran down the stairs and only remembered my fears when I found myself once again going through the dark deserted halls of the basement.

I arrived back in the blood bank just as the timer began to ring. The crossmatch was ready to read. I prepared the samples for microscopic examination, and was peering into the lens of the microscope when a male voice broke the silence. I screamed and turned to see an orderly standing in the doorway.

"Sorry," he laughed. "Didn't mean to startle you."

"Oh God! You scared the hell out of me. It's been one bizarre night."

"Is the blood ready for Third West?"

"Just finishing it. I just have to write up the tags."

The orderly sat down on one of the lab stools and watched as I stamped the requisition and put the tags on the bags of blood.

"Did you bring the specimen down to the lab earlier?" I asked. "The floor usually just sends them down on the dumbwaiter."

"Yes, and normally I would have done that too. There are only two orderlies on duty tonight for the whole hospital, what with the storm and all, so we're really busy but security paged me. Seems he thought he saw a body on a stretcher in the hallway by the blood bank. He couldn't find the orderly from Emerg that took the body down, so he called me. I was on Third West when he called so I thought I might as well bring the specimen down with me."

"Was there a body?"

"No, no body and no stretcher. And it also seems as though there is no security guard now either. I tried to phone him but there was no answer. He's not in his office and not in Emerg."

"That's really spooky," I said, the shivers running up and down my spine. "I don't think I'll be sleeping in the night duty room tonight."

The orderly laughed. "It's not as spooky as all that. He might just be in another part of the hospital. Everyone's so short staffed tonight they're getting anyone they can to run errands."

He picked up one unit of blood, and I watched with regret as he left the lab. I was all alone again.I glanced at the clock. Four thirty. I had a choice of sleeping in the night duty room or sitting up in the emergency ward for the rest of the night. Both thoughts were chilling. I picked up the receiver and left a message with the switchboard that I would be going home. In my panic to get out of the place, I left my winter boots untied and my coat unbuttoned. I switched off the light in the blood bank and prepared to leave. Just as I was about to enter the hallway I heard the squeak of trolley wheels approaching. There were agitated voices. The sounds were coming from the direction of the front of the hospital. I ducked into the dark alcove by the dumbwaiter and held my breath as they passed. They turned the corner just in front of me and headed towards the morgue which what looked like a cadaver. The emergency room nurse was pushing the trolley and the policewoman was walking beside it guiding the front end with one hand. I could only make out snatches of the conversation. The nurse was talking excitedly, "… car accident came in about three am … drunk driver didn't have a scratch on him … other patient D.O.A. … the deceased was the intern's fiancée… intern in denial … in shouting match with the head nurse … orderly took body to the morgue …

half and hour later body turned up back in Emerg … head nurse, orderly and security guard missing. …" They entered the morgue. Almost simultaneously I heard a scream and frantic voices but I couldn't make out what was being said.

I ran down the hallway past the night duty room and the morgue towards the EXIT sign at the end of the hall, pushed open the door to the back parking lot and plunged out into the swirling snow.

I would take my chances with the storm.

I am a Writer

am a writer. Writing compensates for love and relationships that have always led to disappointment and pain. I feel safe in my world of historical fiction. I can manage what happens to the characters in my book. I could never depend on what my partners would choose to do. Yes — partners with an "s".

But one Spring day a real world life opened up for me suddenly and most unexpectedly — a life full of promise, a life that sharpened my senses and made my heart beat faster. All from a routine enquiry about directions. There in the store that day, just when I had given up on love and was asking for directions so I could get to the office before it closed and be on my way back to Victoria, there he was. I didn't realize he was the potential man of my dreams at first. He seemed nice enough but just a man offering directions. I wanted someone in my life, but for me it never worked out well in the end. Two divorces and several heartbreaks later, I shied away from the dating scene and wrapped myself in my own fiction.

I had driven up Island for a meeting at the university. My aunt told me I had a cousin who wrote for the paper. Since I was in town anyway, I thought I would look her up. It was already after four in the afternoon and I couldn't find the place, so I pulled into the little corner store and asked the clerk behind the counter for directions to the newspaper office.

"Which one?"

"I didn't know there was more than one," I said, "but my cousin works there. She writes a daily column and her name is Marilyn."

"I know Marilyn." The voice had a European accent and came from beside a shelf of soup cans. "It's hard to give directions," he said. "It's kind of out of the way, but I can lead you there if you want to follow my car."

Well, he knew my cousin, actually introduced me to her. Then said he would be in Victoria on the weekend and asked if I would like to meet for dinner. My life was about to come alive.

It was early May, and we hit it off splendidly. And with that, I immediately projected the hopes that I had found the perfect partner who I would spend the rest of my life with — and without actually having had to work at it. Every Friday, he sailed down to Victoria where I lived. He had reciprocal mooring at one of the marinas there, and we spent marvelous weekends together, sailing, eating, talking, going to concerts. We both loved classical music. Life was magical. He even stayed one whole week. He worked around my place while I was at work and had dinner ready when I got home. We talked about my selling the house I had just bought and moving into his condo for a trial period to see if we were compatible.

It was my first year at my new job, and in June I spent my three week vacation sailing around the southern gulf islands on his 27 foot Catalina. It was heaven. When I wasn't needed to tack, I sat on the bow of the boat and soaked in the beauty and tranquility of the west coast. After each long wonderfully leisure day of sailing we would pull into the marina, take down the sails and head for the pub. There over a glass of wine (beer for him) we would relax and talk endlessly. We usually ate supper on the deck of the marina but occasionally we bought fresh local seafood and cooked it on the boat. After supper we walked along the dock in the cool evening air watching children peering into the water to marvel at the luminescent jelly fish. A paradise it was — a taste of heaven.

I thought the loneliness was over. One day when I was sitting on the bow, I phoned my very dear and wise friend in the States.

"You deserve this," she said, "after all you've been through. I'm so happy for you."

For the most part, Theodore and I thought very much alike in the terms of the environment, politics, music, art, movies, religion and just life in general. We had both been married twice and through some very painful breakups. There were only a few conversations that went where I didn't want them to. He seemed at times to relish telling me about how he cheated on both of his wives on a continuous basis, and he seemed to think this was to his credit. He seemed to delight in regaling me with his exploits in this regard and seemed offended when I didn't understand him. Those discussions were short though, as I quickly changed the subject. If I had expressed my feelings on the subject we would have had such differences of opinion that we would have been angry with one another. I didn't want to spoil the pleasantness and sheer pleasure of the holiday by quarreling over something that was his business and not mine. A couple of things that would annoy me, which I kept quiet about, was the way he referred to the clerks in the bank where he was a manager as "his girls," and I found the fact that he kept track of them for years after a little bizarre.

Theodore liked to tell me how he "worked his way" through all of "his girls" in the bank, discarding them one by one and moving on to the next of her co-workers. And "women can be catty" as he put it, so there ended up so much discord that the bank transferred him from Victoria to Port Hardy. He "went kicking and screaming" as he had established a wonderful life in the capital city—music, theater and cultured friends. Still in Port Hardy there was a fresh batch of girls to "work his way through." But Theodore's boss "was an ignorant bastard who made his life hell."

Unhappy with his boss and the remote blue collar area he was living in, Theodore managed to get a job teaching finance at a college in a city in the central part of the island, but not before his wife left him.

"She just walked out one day," he said. "We were in the kitchen one late afternoon. She was preparing supper and I was talking on the phone to Stella (the married woman from the bank with whom he was having an affair at the time). Mary [his wife] just laid the potato peeler down on the counter and walked out." His two teenage kids and he " had to go out for supper. The next morning her friend came by for a few of Mary's clothes and told me she wouldn't be coming back."

He seemed baffled by her leaving so I asked, "Why do you think she left?"

"I don't know," he said. "I think she's a lesbian. She moved in with her woman friend when she left."

"Is she still with that woman?"

"No, when their oldest daughter, Lillian, who was living in Vancouver at the time her mother left, bought a house, Mary moved into the basement apartment. You'll get to meet them later when we go over for Leo's (his son's) birthday party."

And I did meet them later that summer. It was late summer, closer to the time Theodore went to Europe for his school reunion. I was a bit uneasy meeting his family for the first time and with their mother being there and all. I thought I would be resented, but that wasn't at all the case. The party was held at his daughter's house and when we came in through the garage, Theodore's son in law and Leo were doing something to the car and Mary had just entered through the door from the house. "This is my son, Leo," Theodore said to me, "and Lillian's husband Ravi." The men looked up from their mechanic job and smiled. Then Theodore launched into an introductory spiel. "And this is Mary who was my first partner in life," he said to me and continued with "and this is Ruth who is my … "

I rolled my eyes. "Oh for heaven's sake, Theodore," I said as I crossed the garage floor and extended my hand to Mary, "I'm Ruth."

She broke into a big smile and said, "I like you."

Later Theodore told me, "Of course she likes you. She's a lesbian."

The family accepted me almost as though they were so used to meeting Theodore's new women they had long since abandoned any feelings of resentment. As a matter of fact, during the meal when Theodore was talking about one of his previous girlfriends, Lillian interrupted to comment, "Dad, you must accumulate a lot of frequent fucker points." To which only Theodore laughed heartily.

Towards the end of our three-week sailing holiday, we sailed into Pender Harbour where we met up with friends of mine. They had sailed down from Nanaimo on their daughter and son-in-law's yacht, a 36 foot Beneteau. Theodore and I were invited for dinner and drinks on their boat and were treated royally. Betty, my friend and best bridge partner, and her husband, Gordon, my lawyer, had become good friends in Calgary. Much to my delight, Theodore turned on his best European charm. He was handsome and debonair and well spoken and of course quite impressed by the Beneteau and expressed the appropriate admiration. Betty was charmed by Theodore's Belgium accent and commented, "I've never known a Belgium that I didn't like." She proceeded to tell Theodore that she had some Belgium blood in her. Her "mother's father was from Dutch Flanders," she said proudly. Well, I didn't flinch and neither did Theodore, but he had told me earlier that the Dutch and French Belgiums were like the Hatfields and McCoys. There was a long running feud between the two districts, a deep running resentment that Theodore brought with him when he immigrated to Canada — that and disdain for the Protestants, he himself being Catholic. I had remarked on first mention of this bias that religion was religion to which he took great umbrage. Those issues could have been a potential source of conflict, but being always a proponent of "pick your battles," I did not think these issues were of great enough importance to me, so I chose to let them drop.

After we left our friend's boat, Theodore scoffed, "Betty puts on airs." He did like Gordon though. And I had to agree somewhat. As much as I liked Betty and enjoyed her friendship — she had so many admirable trait, she was a wonderful mother and grandmother, genuinely concerned about the people in her circle, a great bridge player, intelligent, had a lot of common sense, carried herself with dignity; I can go on and on — she could be an elitist at times. I fit more into Gordon's approach to life. He was involved in social justice issues who "took on too many pro-bono cases" in his criminal law practice according to Betty. They had been married many years and despite this difference of opinion which caused Betty great disappointment (she would have liked their retirement years to be filled with travel and bridge) they had a good marriage and a close knit family. I admired their relationship. It was proof that good relationships don't necessarily involve complete compatibility.

During that virgin trip, I was regaled with stories about his second wife as well. Virginia taught piano and voice and "was a well-sought-after accompanist" at local concerts. She even sang at concerts on occasion and had an incredible soprano voice — "pitch-perfect," he said. He had "fallen in love with her musical talent at once" but needed to court her slowly as she had just recently become widowed, so he began to follow any concert she was in and soon they were married and he moved into the farmhouse where she lived. Together with her property and their combined income, they (given his expressed disdain for farmers and farmhouses, I wondered how much it was "they" and how much it was "he") decided to build a mansion big enough to host concerts in the upscale neighborhood overlooking the water. They bought a prime piece of property —a double lot—and hired a building con-tractor, but for the year the house was being built, Theodore was seconded to a college somewhere in the Middle East which the university was in partnership with. This meant that Mary was left to oversee the construction. That was the year 2001, as Theodore was in the Middle East when the planes flew into the Twin Towers in New York. He said his class cheered at the news, and he feared for his life when he realized how much hatred there was in the room. We talked about that, and it was interesting to hear a first hand account and also the interactions between himself and his colleagues and students. He did have one brief affair with a student there, but that ended abruptly because it was too dangerous for him

— as well he was told he would be sent back to Canada if it continued. He felt very lonely and isolated so he got on an internet dating site and found a girl in one of the countries that boarder Saudi Arabia. I can't remember which country, but suffice it to say she was a "virtuous Muslim woman" who wanted to come to Canada. He brought her to his digs for "conjugal visits" (his words) on occasion, and over the holidays he paid for her to join him on a week long visit to Egypt.

"Why didn't you fly your wife over?" I asked.

The question both exasperated and annoyed him. "Because we were having trouble with the contractors," he retorted, "and she had to be there to take care of things. We almost lost our shirt. The landscapers ran over budget by almost a hundred thousand dollars. A spring was washing out the soil on our steep front lawn and driveway and they had to bring in huge boulders to shore it up and install a drainage system."

Well, on his return to Canada after the first year was complete and the college would not extend his teaching position another year (his "colleagues back-stabbed him with the administration") he planned to bring his mistress—"Ahab the Arab," as I called her much to his indignation. I was a "rabid racist," he said with great contempt — over to Canada. She was the best thing that had ever come into his life and the pain of losing her was the most intense he had ever experienced. Still to that day, he often went down to the Salish Sea and wailed his heart out over her.

His plan was for "Ahab" to live on his boat in Canada while he lived in the mansion on the hill with Virginia. The problem was that "Ahab" did not want to live on the boat. She wanted him to get a divorce and they (Theodore and she) could live in the mansion. At any rate, she could not get into Canada, only into the States. So Theodore flew her to her brother's place in California, and from there bused her to Seattle. He then snuck away from home on the pretense of going sailing by himself. He moored in Friday Harbour on San Juan Island and took the ferry over to Seattle to meet her. He had planned on spending the summer sailing around the Southern Gulf Islands but "Ahab" didn't like boats. She wouldn't even get on a ferry. So he rented a car and they stayed in motels and toured Washington state. It was beautiful but it "just about bankrupted him." So it didn't work out that well for him, and she married an older American man a short while after her return to her homeland and is now living in the States.

Well after our sailing holiday we talked about possibly living together. After all, if you can spend three weeks confined to the cramped quarters of a 27 foot sailboat and still be talking to one another, we must be compatible. My contract at work was up the end of September and we planned to sail up to Desolation Sound. It is a favorite spot for sailers and incredibly beautiful. But the other thing he wanted to do was to go back and visit Belgium one last time. The private school he attended in Brussels was holding its 50 year reunion and his best friend would be there from South Africa. But he couldn't afford to do both.

"Go to your reunion," I said. " We can do Desolation Sound next year."

Well he really wanted to go to Desolation Sound. It wasn't until late summer, the weekend after the tiff we had in Victoria one day when I called him an asshole. That is really a terrible thing to say to somebody, but it just slipped out of my mouth. He was *tres* insulted, but I apologized and the rest of the weekend went smoothly but by the following weekend, he had decided to go to the school reunion after all. It was after we returned from the concert that night (I drove up island after work that Friday) that he told me. That was fine with me. I needed to get unpacked and do some things around the house that I had put on hold so that I could spend weekends with him. But over the weeks to come, I began to notice a few things — an email that was open on his computer when I walked into his office and draped myself around the back of his neck to tell him lunch was served. The email was from a woman who he explained he had dated many years ago before he came to Canada. "Just a friend," he said. When I asked why she signed off with "Love," he said that was just how she talked. Still there were other things that made me think that possibly he wasn't being completely honest. We sailed over to Salt Spring Island the weekend before he was to leave for Belgium, tied up in Ganges harbor and spent the weekend hiking in Mount Maxwell Provincial Park, taking meals at Moby Dick pub or barbecuing on the boat. It was wonderful, but somehow I wondered if he was planning to meet a woman in Belgium. It didn't seem like he was actually going to miss me like I was going to miss him.

"It wasn't necessary for me to take Tuesday off work to take him to the airport in Vancouver and see him off," he told me. I said it was no problem, I was actually looking forward to it and wanted to be with him right up until his plane lifted off Canadian soil. But he didn't seem to share the ache that was in my heart that we would be apart for three whole weeks. (It had originally only been ten days) He wasn't going to stay with me Monday night either. He would go over to Vancouver after I left for work in the morning and stay with his daughter and she would take him to the airport the next day. I only learned of these plan changes that Sunday. I felt hurt. I had a feeling that he had made these changes to the plans much earlier but put off telling me until this last minute.

So I confronted him. "Theodore," I said when we were sitting at the peak of Mount Maxwell soaking up the mountain air and incredible west coast scenery, "I have to tell you that I was never impressed with the way you constantly cheated on both your wives. Perhaps it is who you are, and your wives must have accepted that to some degree for your marriages to last so long. But I have to tell you that that is not something I am prepared to tolerate."

He tried to dismiss the subject but I said, "I have to say this to you because I'm wondering if you have someone you plan to see when you're in Belgium. Perhaps someone you met on the internet or someone you would like to rekindle a relationship with. Of course, you have every right in the world to be intimate with whoever you choose. I don't own you. But I have every right to end our relationship ." I said, "I need to know because if that is the case we should sever ties before you go. Then if it doesn't work out for you and I am still available and willing, and there is a good chance that that may be the case, we can pick up where we left off."

"No, definitely not," he said, "there is nothing like that."

And with that he went to Belgium — he full of excitement and anticipation and me full of sadness and anxiety.

For the next few days, he called every day and talked for an hour (he thought he had a cell phone plan that only charged him ten cents a minute and was shocked when they shut off his phone when the phone bill hit $2000.00) so after that he sent long emails about how he missed me and about how lonely he was and about his old classmates. I was relieved. Perhaps I had been wrong. I busied myself fixing my house up, exercising and dieting and shopping for clothes and counting the days until his return. But for the last week, I received nothing. I emailed him every day but got nothing in return. I even tried phoning him but the phone had been discontinued. I thought I would hear from him at least the day he left Belgium. He had planned to take a seaplane from the Vancouver airport to Victoria where I was to pick him up.. I awaited his call with great anticipation. The house was immaculate, I had lost five pounds, looked good in my new clothes, hors d'oeuvres were ready in the fridge and the bottle of his favorite wine waited to be opened, but the call never came. Then a couple of hours after the plane was to have landed, the call came in. He couldn't talk long but "just wanted to let me know that he had phoned Ardith (a previous girlfriend who lived in Vancouver) to pick him up at the airport and drive him to the Horseshoe Bay ferry. He would be down to see me on the weekend. Couldn't talk now as they had an accident as they were leaving the airport and were pressed to make the last ferry in time. He would reinsert the chip in his phone and call me from the ferry.

I was completely shaken. Waiting for Theodore's call was agony, so I phoned a friend from a past failed relationship of mine, a man I had lived with for six months in Calgary. I knew better than to call him, better than to send out any positive vibes at all that I might be inclined to rekindle that relationship, but I felt so desperate. Peter was accommodatingly nice and offered welcome advice. "Theodore is using your hurt to bolster his ego," he said. "When he calls tell him to keep on trucking. It's over." And I did just that. I paced the floor waiting for the phone to ring and when it did, I feigned a matter-of-fact attitude and told him just that, to keep on trucking, we were through and I hung up. I didn't answer his next call and that gave me a little bit of comfort. His message

(I let the call — his name came up on caller display— go into voicemail) said he was jet lagged and tired when he landed in Vancouver and just wanted to go to his own home after being away for three weeks and get rested and unpacked. He didn't call again until late the next afternoon.

I had a hard time not answering his persistent apologetic voice messages and emails, so when my contract ended I went over to the Sunshine Coast to visit my cousin for a week. That way I didn't hear the phone ringing and know it was him, I didn't have access to email and I wasn't alone with my thoughts. By the time I returned home, he had stopped trying to contact me. I erased everything from him, gained twenty pounds and started writing.

That was the last relationship I had. Well, except for the man I met in Spain on the Camino, but he told me he was married. Well, not until after the two week long relationship and we slept together. He told me the next morning after breakfast just before he left to return home to Toronto Ontario.

I visited the maritimes this summer. I wanted to talk to my friends about the new book I am writing about the Stone Age megalithic builders of Old Europe. It is a world where the characters I create make sense to me. But my friends interrupt and ask about me.

"You should forget about historical fiction," they said. "You need to write about your life."

"I can't," I responded. "I really can't go there."

I write historical fiction.

About the Author

Ruth Welburn has written two children's books, two historical fiction and many short stories and magazine and newspaper articles.

Bedbug's Big Adventure: the way of Saint James and *Road to the Ocean* are the only books written about the Camino for children.

The Devil's Ruse was published in 2010. It is set in 1918 at the end of the Great War and details events leading up to and during the pandemic.

Land of the Watchers: the lost civilization of Stonehenge is completed and soon to be published.

Retired from the field of medical research, she lives on beautiful Vancouver Island where she combines her love of research with writing.